About This Book

Why is this topic important?

Keeping customers satisfied with the service they receive helps an organization build and foster a valuable reputation for dependability and quality performance. The results of service-based interactions directly influence the perception that the customer has of the product or service and the company itself. It is vital to help employees develop service strategies that create a positive image, communicate effectively, and build customer rapport to support the underlying values and beliefs of an organization.

What can you achieve with this book?

You can help make your company's customer service sizzle with *101 Ways to Improve Customer Service: Training, Tools, Tips, and Techniques.* This book provides a variety of training and development interventions that can be used immediately with frontline service employees. It is intended to be a user-friendly guide to developing and sharpening the skills necessary to provide excellent care to customers, both inside and outside the organization.

How is this book organized?

This book contains 50 training activities, 14 tools, 23 tips, and 14 techniques that encompass 6 different categories: Awareness, Communication, Planning, Problem Solving, Quality, and Teamwork. A topical index aids in selecting appropriate interventions, and 4 appendixes list recommended interventions for the challenging environments of internal customers, call centers, retail, and sales. The book also contains a CD-ROM with training handouts and tools that are fully reproducible.

About Pfeiffer

Pfeiffer serves the professional development and hands-on resource needs of training and human resource practitioners and gives them products to do their jobs better. We deliver proven ideas and solutions from experts in HR development and HR management, and we offer effective and customizable tools to improve workplace performance. From novice to seasoned professional, Pfeiffer is the source you can trust to make yourself and your organization more successful.

Essential Knowledge Pfeiffer produces insightful, practical, and comprehensive materials on topics that matter the most to training and HR professionals. Our Essential Knowledge resources translate the expertise of seasoned professionals into practical, how-to guidance on critical workplace issues and problems. These resources are supported by case studies, worksheets, and job aids and are frequently supplemented with CD-ROMs, websites, and other means of making the content easier to read, understand, and use.

Essential Tools Pfeiffer's Essential Tools resources save time and expense by offering proven, ready-to-use materials—including exercises, activities, games, instruments, and assessments—for use during a training or team-learning event. These resources are frequently offered in looseleaf or CD-ROM format to facilitate copying and customization of the material.

Pfeiffer also recognizes the remarkable power of new technologies in expanding the reach and effectiveness of training. While e-hype has often created whizbang solutions in search of a problem, we are dedicated to bringing convenience and enhancements to proven training solutions. All our e-tools comply with rigorous functionality standards. The most appropriate technology wrapped around essential content yields the perfect solution for today's on-the-go trainers and human resource professionals.

Pfeiffer
www.pfeiffer.com   *Essential resources for training and HR professionals*

Pfeiffer™

Lorraine L. Ukens

101 Ways to Improve Customer Service

Training, Tools, Tips, and Techniques

BICENTENNIAL
1807
WILEY
2007
BICENTENNIAL

John Wiley & Sons, Inc.

Cataloging-in-Publication Data on file with the Library of Congress.
ISBN-13: 978-0-7879-8200-3

Acquiring Editor: Martin Delahoussaye
Director of Development: Kathleen Dolan Davies
Production Editor: Nina Kreiden
Editor: Michele D. Jones

Manufacturing Supervisor: Becky Carreño
Editorial Assistant: Julie Rodriguez
Interior Design: Gene Crofts

Printed in the United States of America
Printing   10 9 8 7 6 5 4 3 2 1

Contents

Contents for the CD-ROM   xvii

Introduction: Getting the Most from This Resource   1

Topical Index of Interventions   9

section ONE

Awareness   13

training 1

Collection Inspection: Observation   15

training 2

Conjecture Lecture: First Impressions   17

training 3

Information, Please: Observation and Information Gathering   21

training 4

It's a Jungle out There: Stereotyping   23

training 5

Just My Luck: Personal Perspective   27

training 6

Making Sense of It: Sensory Acuity   33

training 7
    See Saw: Visual Perception   37

training 8
    Stressing the Positive: Workplace Stressors   41

training 9
    What Now? Perceptual Expectations   47

tool 10
    On the Line: Credibility   51

tool 11
    Power Up: Assertiveness   53

tip 12
    Flex Your Mind: Mental Flexibility   57

tip 13
    Keep It Cool: Job Pressure   59

tip 14
    Stress Buster: Stress Reduction   61

technique 15
    Meltdown: Dealing with Anger   63

technique 16
    Plead Your Case: Influencing Change   65

section TWO

Communication   67

training 17
    Blueprints for Success: Verbal Instructions   69

training 18
From Me to You: Focus on Others 71

training 19
Negative Ten-dency: Word Usage 75

training 20
Poker Face: Nonverbal Communication 79

training 21
Say What You Mean: Concise Verbal Communication 85

training 22
Seeing Is Believing: Body Language and Culture 89

training 23
Summary Judgment: Listening 93

training 24
Tongue-Tying Twisters: Word Enunciation 95

tool 25
Listen Closely: Responsive Listening 99

tool 26
Mind the Message: Communication Processes 101

tool 27
Probing Points: Questioning 105

tool 28
Sound Advice: Voice Quality 109

tip 29
Crossing the Border: International Communication 111

tip 30
    E-Service: Electronic Communication   113

technique 31
    Attention, Please: Keeping the Customer's Attention   115

technique 32
    Return Policy: Feedback Guidelines   117

technique 33
    Six Degrees of Persuasion: Influencing Through Listening   119

section **THREE**

Planning   121

training 34
    Color Quest: Limited Resources   123

training 35
    Commercial Appeal: Product or Service Offerings   125

training 36
    Flow Motion: Work Process Improvement   127

training 37
    Hardware: Classifying Resources   131

training 38
    Heads and Tails: Optimizing Resources   135

training 39
    Last Straw: Goal Setting and Resources   139

training 40
    On Target: Goal Alignment 143

training 41
    View from the Top: Personal Change Management 147

tool 42
    Desk Stress: Organization 149

tool 43
    Pass It On: Delegation 153

tip 44
    Flag It: File Management 155

tip 45
    Just the Fax: Fax Information File 157

tip 46
    Library Dues: Development Resources 159

tip 47
    Memory Ticklers: Information Recall 161

tip 48
    New Kids on the Block: Orientation 163

tip 49
    To Do or Not to Do: To-Do Lists 165

technique 50
    Setting the Bar: Service Standards 167

technique 51
    Tackling Time Wasters: Time Management 169

section FOUR

Problem Solving   173

training 52
Comic Relief: Analyzing Problem Situations   175

training 53
Dialing Dilemma: Telephone Logic Problem   179

training 54
It's All in How You Look at It: Problem Interpretation   183

training 55
Medical Breakthrough: Logical Problem Analysis   187

training 56
Miss Interpretation: Problem Interpretation   193

training 57
Nominally Speaking: Nominal Group Technique   195

training 58
Role It Out: Situational Role Play   199

training 59
Sensible Solutions: Alternative Solutions   205

tool 60
Breaking Barriers: Obstacles to Problem Solving   207

tool 61
Creativity Quotient: Self-Assessment   211

tip 62
A CAP-ital Idea: Creative Action Planning   215

tip 63
   Feelings Check-In: Conflict Reaction Assessment   217

tip 64
   Share to Be Aware: Interdepartmental Problem Solving   219

technique 65
   Crash Control: Conflict Management Styles   221

technique 66
   Fair Play: Win-Win Negotiation   225

technique 67
   Stage Right: Creative Process   229

section **FIVE**

Quality   231

training 68
   Getting the Word Out: Quality Components   233

training 69
   Inconvenience Store: Service Strategies   237

training 70
   Like It or Not: Service Analogies   239

training 71
   Making the Connection: Customer Expectations   245

training 72
   Overcharged and Underrated: Exceeding Expectations   249

training 73
   Picture Perfect: Communicating Quality   253

training 74
   RATER of the Lost Art: Customer Perception of Quality   257

training 75
   Right Approach: Service Attitude   261

training 76
   Service Link: Creative Analysis of Service   265

tool 77
   Cream of the Crop: Quality Competencies   269

tool 78
   May I Help You? Telephone Etiquette   273

tip 79
   Behind the Scenes: Support Role Recognition   277

tip 80
   Getting Down to Business: Customer Comment Cards   279

tip 81
   Hit the Heights: Customer Service Week   281

tip 82
   Knowledge Is Power: Technical Training   283

technique 83
   Concession Stand: Acknowledging Customer Concerns   285

technique 84
   Write On: Letters of Complaint   287

section SIX

Teamwork 289

training 85
Candy Land: Group Decision Making 291

training 86
In and Out: Internal Customers 295

training 87
Mind the Details: Individual vs. Team Performance 299

training 88
On Course: Communication, Reliability, and Trust 303

training 89
Open Account: Team Environment 307

training 90
Port of Call: Partnering Strategies 313

training 91
Seeing STARS: Group Interdependence 315

training 92
To the Letter: Time-Constrained Team Performance 325

tool 93
A Matter of Trust: Team Member Trust 329

tool 94
Team Checkup: Group Effectiveness 333

tip 95
Bank on It: Peer Recognition 337

tip 96
Get on Board: Peer Feedback   339

tip 97
Rely on Me: Team Trust   341

tip 98
Rivalry or Revelry: Constructive Competition   343

tip 99
Team Talent: Resource Directory   345

technique 100
Confront with Care: Team Conflict Management   347

technique 101
Opposition Position: Constructive Competition   349

Appendix A: Internal Customer Service   351
Appendix B: Call Centers   355
Appendix C: Retail   357
Appendix D: Sales   359
About the Author   363
How to Use the CD-ROM   365

Contents for the CD-ROM

section ONE

Awareness

training 2
> Conjecture Lecture Worksheet

training 4
> It's a Jungle out There Worksheet

training 5
> Just My Luck Fortune Slips
> Just My Luck Worksheet

training 6
> Making Sense of It Instruction Sheet

training 8
> Stressing the Positive Checklist
> Stressing the Positive Worksheet

training 9
> What Now? Worksheet

tool 10
> On the Line: Credibility

tool 11
>   Power Up: Assertiveness

tip 12
>   Flex Your Mind: Mental Flexibility

tip 13
>   Keep It Cool: Job Pressure

tip 14
>   Stress Buster: Stress Reduction

technique 15
>   Meltdown: Dealing with Anger

technique 16
>   Plead Your Case: Influencing Change

section TWO

Communication

training 19
>   Negative Ten-dency Worksheet

training 20
>   Poker Face Role Cards
>   Poker Face Hand Rankings Sheet

training 21
>   Say What You Mean Instruction Sheet

training 24
>   Tongue-Tying Twisters Handout

tool 25
>   Listen Closely: Responsive Listening

tool 26
> Mind the Message: Communication Processes

tool 27
> Probing Points: Questioning

tool 28
> Sound Advice: Voice Quality

tip 29
> Crossing the Border: International Communication

tip 30
> E-Service: Electronic Communication

technique 31
> Attention, Please: Keeping the Customer's Attention

technique 32
> Return Policy: Feedback Guidelines

technique 33
> Six Degrees of Persuasion: Influencing Through Listening

section THREE

Planning

training 36
> Flow Motion Worksheet

training 38
> Heads and Tails Answer Sheet

training 39
> Last Straw Requisition Form

training 40

On Target Worksheet

tool 42

Desk Stress: Organization

tool 43

Pass It On: Delegation

tip 44

Flag It: File Management

tip 45

Just the Fax: Fax Information File

tip 46

Library Dues: Development Resources

tip 47

Memory Ticklers: Information Recall

tip 48

New Kids on the Block: Orientation

tip 49

To Do or Not to Do: To-Do Lists

technique 50

Setting the Bar: Service Standards

technique 51

Tackling Time Wasters: Time Management

section FOUR

Problem Solving

training 52
>   Comic Relief Worksheet

training 53
>   Dialing Dilemma Worksheet

training 55
>   Medical Breakthrough Worksheet
>   Medical Breakthrough Solution Sheet

training 57
>   Nominally Speaking Worksheet

training 58
>   Role It Out Information Sheet
>   Role It Out Situations Sheet
>   Role It Out Recommended Actions Sheet

tool 60
>   Breaking Barriers: Obstacles to Problem Solving

tool 61
>   Creativity Quotient: Self-Assessment

tip 62
>   A CAP-ital Idea: Creative Action Planning

tip 63
>   Feelings Check-In: Conflict Reaction Assessment

tip 64
>   Share to Be Aware: Interdepartmental Problem Solving

technique 65

Crash Control: Conflict Management Styles

technique 66

Fair Play: Win-Win Negotiation

technique 67

Stage Right: Creative Process

section FIVE

Quality

training 68

Getting the Word Out Worksheet

training 70

Like It or Not Worksheets

training 71

Making the Connection Worksheet

training 72

Overcharged and Underrated Role-Play Sheet

training 74

RATER of the Lost Art Information Sheet

training 75

Right Approach Worksheet

training 76

Service Link Game Board

tool 77

Cream of the Crop: Quality Competencies

tool 78
>   May I Help You? Telephone Etiquette

tip 79
>   Behind the Scenes: Support Role Recognition

tip 80
>   Getting Down to Business: Customer Comment Cards

tip 81
>   Hit the Heights: Customer Service Week

tip 82
>   Knowledge Is Power: Technical Training

technique 83
>   Concession Stand: Acknowledging Customer Concerns

technique 84
>   Write On: Letters of Complaint

section SIX

Teamwork

training 85
>   Candy Land Worksheet
>   Candy Land Answer Sheet

training 86
>   In and Out Worksheet

training 87
>   Mind the Details Worksheet

training 89
>   Open Account Picture Cards

training 91
     Seeing STARS Cards
     Seeing STARS Card Sets Answer Sheet

training 92
     To the Letter Worksheet

tool 93
     A Matter of Trust: Team Member Trust

tool 94
     Team Checkup: Group Effectiveness

tip 95
     Bank on It: Peer Recognition

tip 96
     Get on Board: Peer Feedback

tip 97
     Rely on Me: Team Trust

tip 98
     Rivalry or Revelry: Constructive Competition

tip 99
     Team Talent: Resource Directory

technique 100
     Confront with Care: Team Conflict Management

technique 101
     Opposition Position: Constructive Competition

Introduction
Getting the Most from This Resource

PURPOSE

This is a collection of 101 practical applications (50 training activities, 14 tools, 23 tips, and 14 techniques) to improve the frontline employee's ability to provide exceptional customer service. It is intended to be a down-to-earth guide to giving excellent care to customers, both inside and outside the organization. It covers the many topical areas that encompass customer service and is organized to be user-friendly.

Customer service representatives are vital to any business because they serve a major role as liaison between the customer and the company. The results of these interactions directly influence the perception that the customer has of the product or service and the company itself. The attitude and actions of service providers will cause a customer to make a perceptual judgment about the company. From the customer's perspective, the people performing the service *are* the company.

More and more, the word is being spread about the need for organizations to develop a corporate culture that extols quality products and service. This message is accompanied by endless anecdotes of customer experiences and why it is necessary to constantly strive for improvement. Although management leadership, support, and involvement clearly are important, training and skills development still play a critical role in any successful service improvement effort. Learning to create a positive image, communicate effectively, and build customer rapport gives employees the means to develop quality service strategies that support the underlying values and beliefs of their organization.

Keeping customers satisfied with the service they receive helps an organization build and foster a valuable reputation for dependability and quality performance. We know that the customer's perception of service is fundamental to his or her degree of satisfaction, and the practical meaning of good service extends far beyond technical excellence. Providing quality service requires the ability to remain flexible and respond to the changing conditions and needs of the customer.

Service representatives must have a combination of good interpersonal skills, competent knowledge of the business or occupation, and proficient problem-solving abilities. Understanding customer expectations and the basic components of customer service helps employees build these appropriate skill sets. It is wise to remember that the average customer is educated, knowledgeable, time driven, value-oriented, opinionated, and skeptical. A solid service quality plan is as critical to a successful improvement effort as a good map is to a successful journey. Satisfying customers through high-level service helps build and foster a valuable reputation for dependability and quality performance. It also strengthens customer loyalty, which means continued business with the organization.

When employees are given the proper training and support, they are provided the necessary tools to achieve success. This collection of training activities, assessment tools, practical tips, and recommended techniques will provide a variety of opportunities to strengthen the capabilities and effectiveness of customer service representatives. They are designed to challenge employees to beat their personal best and constantly strive to improve skills and output. Remember, a properly trained and well-informed staff will help deliver a winning performance that keeps both internal and external customers satisfied. These interventions will help them stay focused, enthusiastic, motivated, and efficient.

AUDIENCE

These interventions can be implemented by trainers, team leaders, or managers for employees who provide service to external customers as well as those internal to an organization. Organizational development practitioners also may find this resource valuable in enhancing the basic interpersonal skills of all employees.

The training activities include all processing information, and the facilitator guidelines presented in this Introduction provide the appropriate support for team leaders and managers to conduct the training sessions.

PRODUCT DESCRIPTION

There are four types of interventions included in this book:

1. *Training:* hands-on activities with reflective discussions (includes detailed processing instructions, worksheets, and debriefing questions)

2. *Tools:* questionnaires, checklists, and assessments for individuals and groups

3. *Tips:* brief ideas and recommended actions to be implemented by individuals or leaders

4. *Techniques:* guidelines, process models, and strategies for use by individuals or leaders

The content is divided into six sections, representing various categories of customer service skills, and each section provides basic information on how the category relates to the overall concept of quality service. The sections are as follows:

1. *Awareness:* assessing one's personal strengths as well as exploring how personal perspective affects perception and behavior

2. *Communication:* examining how things are communicated through verbal and nonverbal processes

3. *Planning:* focusing on structure, preparation, and management in terms of task completion, which includes knowledge, work organization, documentation, use of available resources, and continuous improvement efforts

4. *Problem solving:* using creativity and logic skills as well as coping with difficulties that present problems in work situations

5. *Quality:* examining the ability to know customers and their needs, exceed expectations, and provide added value to enhance service

6. *Teamwork:* relying on cooperation and interdependence within and among individuals or groups

Many of the interventions can be applied in different topical areas, and a topical index is included at the front of the book to help in the selection of appropriate interventions. In addition, appendixes have been included to list the interventions that are highly recommended for four specific areas within customer service environments that may pose special challenges for service providers: internal customers, call centers, retail, and sales. The book contains a CD-ROM, and all training handouts and tools are fully reproducible.

● ●

KEY TERMS

Collaboration   The ability to work together to produce an integrated joint effort, such as found in the concept of teamwork

Conflict   Differences among ideas, perceptions, beliefs, and goals of individuals

Creativity   The ability to be inventive, imaginative, or original

Empathy   Identification with and understanding of another's situation, feelings, and motives

External customer   The recipient of services outside the organization

Internal customer   The recipient of services that are bounded within the confines of the organization

Intervention   Any action introduced into a situation so as to alter an outcome or development

Negotiation   The reciprocal bargaining process that is a basis of agreement between opposing parties

Partnering   A win-win collaboration between two or more parties

Perception   The view individuals have of things in the world around them and its effect on concept formation and behavior

Resource utilization   The interpretation of data and information, as well as the use of available supplies and workforce

Stereotyping   Making cognitive generalizations about the qualities and characteristics of the members of a particular group

Trust   Confidence in the integrity, ability, character, and truth of an individual or process

• •

FACILITATOR GUIDELINES FOR TRAINING ACTIVITIES

The training activities are designed to stimulate discussion and learning by actively engaging all participants in the process. Because participants draw on their personal experiences, these hands-on exercises can help illustrate, emphasize, or summarize points in a very effective way. Although each training activity is presented within a specific category, the flexible nature of experiential games allows for most of them to be applied within several different content areas.

The four types of interventions (training, tools, tips, techniques) are presented to complement one another so that they can be used in combination. That is, the facilitator may begin a training session with an assessment tool, followed by one or two training activities that are transitioned with some recommended technique(s) that can be used in application to the job. The tips support the training within the work environment to keep the message up front on an ongoing and practical basis and may be intended for application by either individual service representatives or the team leader.

Group Size and Time Required

Group size and amount of time available are both considerations that will affect the facilitator's choice of training activities. The exercises presented are very flexible and can accommodate a variety of group sizes and time constraints. The specified time required is an approximation, as the actual length of the exercise depends on several factors—for example, the number of participants and the extent and style of the debriefing session. A general guideline to follow is that the larger the group, the longer the time required. It may be necessary to adjust a specific activity to meet personal conditions by reducing or extending the amount of "play" during a timed activity or the discussion period (or both). Remember, however, that the activity is the vehicle for the learning process that occurs during the debriefing, so be careful to find a comfortable balance of play and discussion, not sacrificing one segment for the other.

Facilitator's Role

The facilitator's role is to help participants make the connection between the training experience and the intent of the learning. There needs to be a good match between the metaphors of the event and real-life issues. The activity itself must be set up, run, and processed with a link to the real world. When using games and entertaining activities to teach a lesson, the facilitator must underscore the instructional message behind the fun so that participants take the training seriously. Therefore, the debriefing is an especially critical point in the overall process. The facilitator leads people to insights by discussing, reflecting on, and questioning what was experienced. Rather than telling the learning points of the exercise, an effective leader should guide participants into awareness.

Unless an activity calls for the facilitator to take an active role, participants should be allowed to experience the event on their own. They should be allowed the freedom to make mistakes because this in itself is an excellent way to examine the situation and learn from its outcomes. The facilitator should intervene only on questions of procedure and only to give as much detail as possible to answer the inquiries without influencing results.

Debriefing an Activity

The debriefing or feedback session is the most important step in making the connection between the activity and what is to be learned from it. Discussion questions and background information specific to its various applications have been provided with each activity. Select those questions that are most relevant to the chosen topic of the training session within the time available for discussion.

The questions presented in the activities are intended to guide participants in seeing the relevance of the event within the context of the objective. They are by no means inclusive, and the facilitator should feel free to add others. Remember that participant feedback during the debriefing session may lead to other areas of discussion not specifically included here. It is important to address those issues appropriate to the topic and to shelve those subjects that take the discussion off track.

Selection of Interventions

The interventions can be applied to a variety of situations. A topical index is provided on page 9 to help the facilitator select appropriate interventions for a variety of different topics within the six categories of customer service that are presented.

A training activity may be used alone as the main learning event, or several exercises may be used within a training session to reinforce or introduce any number of topics. For any given topic, there are a variety of exercises that differ in complexity and in the demands made of the participants. Don't forget to evaluate the needs of your own customers—the training participants—and select activities that are most suitable for the intended audience.

The tips are intended to be used by the individual service provider or a team leader to create the customer service infrastructure. The tools and techniques may be used as stand-alone interventions, or they can be added as support material for topics discussed during training sessions. Unless otherwise noted, the tools and techniques can be used by either an individual or a team leader. Facilitator notes have been provided with each tool to make specific recommendations for its most effective use.

●●●●●●●●●●●●●●●●●●●●●●●●●●●●●●●

RESOURCES

Books

Albrecht, K. (1995). *At America's service: How your company can join the customer service revolution.* New York: Warner Books.

Blanchard, K. (1993). *Raving fans: A revolutionary approach to customer service.* New York: Morrow.

Disney Institute. (2003). *Perfecting the art of customer service.* New York: Disney Editions.

Schwarz, R. (1994). *The skilled facilitator.* San Francisco: Jossey-Bass.

Snow, D., & Yanovitch, T. (2003). *Unleashing excellence: The complete guide to ultimate customer service.* Sanford, FL: DC Press.

Ury, W. (1993). *Getting past no: Negotiating your way from confrontation to cooperation* (2nd ed.). New York: Bantam Books.

Zemke, R., & Anderson, K. (2003). *Delivering knock your socks off service* (3rd ed.). New York: AMACOM.

Zemke, R., & Woods, J. A. (Eds.). (1999). *Best practices in customer service.* New York: AMACOM.

Websites

American Productivity and Quality Center (www.apqc.org)

Association of Support Professionals (www.asponline.com)

Customer Service Group (www.customserservicegroup.com)

Institute of Customer Service (www.instituteofcustomerservice.com)

International Customer Service Association (www.icsa.com)

Service and Support Professionals Association (www.thesspa.com)

Topical Index of Interventions

Angry customer   15, 83, 84

Assertiveness   11, 15, 16, 33

Body language   6, 20, 22

Change   12, 16, 32, 33, 34, 38, 39, 41

Collaboration   24, 34, 55, 62, 66, 79, 87, 91, 92, 94, 99, 101

Communication process   7, 17, 18, 19, 26, 88, 89

Competition   37, 39, 91, 98, 101

Conflict   15, 19, 63, 65, 67, 100

Consensus   66, 74, 85

Continuous improvement   23, 28, 36, 37, 39, 46, 64, 69, 80, 90

Creativity   9, 12, 35, 39, 56, 57, 61, 62, 67, 69, 73, 76, 89

Credibility   6, 10, 16, 20, 93, 97

Decision making   3, 52, 57, 59, 60, 74, 85

Delegation   43

Diversity   22, 29, 63, 73, 89

Documentation   44, 45, 49

Empathy   15, 18, 69, 74, 83

Empowerment   43, 46, 82

Expectations   2, 9, 35, 40, 63, 66, 68, 70, 71, 72, 74, 77, 80, 88

Feedback   32, 43, 48, 80, 82, 96

Fun   13, 14, 81, 96, 98

Goals   34, 39, 40, 50

Information gathering   3, 17, 27, 64, 99

Learning   43, 46, 48, 82

Listening   15, 17, 21, 23, 25, 31, 32, 33, 85

Logic   16, 38, 53, 55, 76

Memory   1, 47

Mind-set   12, 16, 56

Motivation   40, 81, 95, 96, 98, 101

Negotiation   11, 33, 34, 66

Observation   1, 3, 6, 7, 20, 22, 58, 87

Organization   42, 45, 47, 49

Orientation   48, 94

Partnering   43, 58, 64, 79, 81, 86, 88, 89, 90, 94, 95, 97

Perception   5, 7, 9, 12, 16, 19, 22, 25, 54, 56, 63, 73, 74, 76, 89

Personal interaction   4, 6, 15, 18, 20, 22, 26, 32, 65, 83, 93, 100

Persuasion   16, 31, 33, 73

Problem statements   52, 54, 56

Problem-solving process   44, 52, 53, 55, 57, 59, 60, 62, 66, 76, 91

Procedures   17, 36, 37, 47, 50, 69, 72, 90, 92

Professionalism   10, 15, 77, 83, 97, 100

Recognition   79, 81, 95, 98

Resource utilization   34, 37, 38, 39, 87, 99

Solving customer problems   15, 44, 58, 80, 83, 84

Solving team problems   8, 36, 51, 57, 63, 64, 89, 99, 100

Standards   36, 50, 77, 78, 82, 89

Stereotyping   2, 4

Strategic planning   34, 38, 39, 64

Stress   8, 13, 14, 43, 51

Telephone   31, 53, 78

Time management   45, 49, 51, 55, 91, 92

Trust   10, 16, 20, 42, 88, 93, 97

Verbal communication   7, 11, 15, 17, 19, 21, 23, 24, 25, 26, 28, 29, 32, 78, 88

Viewpoint   4, 16, 18, 33, 41, 54, 56, 63, 75, 76

Voice   24, 28

Written communication   19, 30, 73, 84

Awareness

Awareness of the personal view he or she has of self, other people, and the environment creates a certain perspective that affects how a service representative performs a job, interacts with customers, and reacts to situations. Because these individuals often carry the weight of how a customer might evaluate the entire organization, it is imperative that they stay attuned to their capabilities and attitudes.

The service representative plays a major role as liaison between the customer and the company. The results of these interactions directly influence the perception that the customer has of the product or service and the company itself. Perception is an individual's personal understanding or view of things in the world, and perception is a large part of how expectations are formed. Service providers base their impressions of customers on their interactions with them, and customers base their judgments about the company on the attitude and actions of service representatives.

A perceptual set is a person's tendency to see things in a certain way, do things a certain way, and stick to the familiar because it's more comfortable than changing. Service providers need to be aware of their own perceptual sets as well as those of coworkers and customers. This will help them accept other points of view and overcome assumptions that influence decisions. Service providers' mind-sets play another critical role in customer service in that they affect customer expectations. If employees can see things the way customers see them, they have a chance to make inroads in helping customers change their mind-sets.

Service providers must learn to see things from the customer's perspective. In this way, they can understand the nature of customer expectations and then focus on what they can do to help make the service transaction a positive one. Interactions can be improved by understanding that people have different viewpoints, identifying and avoiding potential causes for misinterpretations, learning to separate fact from inference, and checking the accuracy of personal perceptions. A major step in acquiring this understanding occurs through accurate observation of people, things, and events.

Stereotypes are often applied to connect certain characteristics or abilities to people. These individual perceptions are based on personal opinions and value systems, and they can influence interactions with others, whether consciously or unconsciously. In today's global marketplace, service providers encounter a high degree of customer diversity. Customers are unique in their beliefs and feelings, and circumstances affect the meaning of how situations are perceived. In order to respond to diverse demands, service providers have to get to know their own customers and their specific needs.

Service representatives also must handle the inherent frustrations of heavy customer contact and remain calm in demanding situations. Stress reduction strategies can help change either personal viewpoint or the work environment itself. Adding some relaxation and fun to the workday can help lighten spirits and reduce stress. Taking a lighthearted look at situations can put some of the most difficult problems into perspective.

Service representatives need to recognize their own skill sets and unique talents, as well as those of their teammates, so that these assets can be properly utilized to provide the highest quality service possible. Finally, it is imperative that service representatives communicate a professional image and build good rapport with both customers and associates. Individuals should be able to assert control of situations so that they can communicate their thoughts, feelings, and beliefs in a direct, honest, and appropriate way. These efforts will improve service representatives' credibility and trustworthiness.

Collection Inspection

Observation

Goal
To stimulate skills of observation. Participants will observe a container of items and then list the items from memory.

Time Required
Approximately 20 to 30 minutes

Group Size
Subgroups of three to five persons each, with a maximum of twenty-five participants

Materials

- One small opaque container with lid and an assortment of twenty-five different small items for each subgroup, to include such things as buttons, poker chips, marbles, pencils, stamps, washers, pins, thumbtacks, and so on (*Note:* Each subgroup should have an identical set of items.)

- One sheet of blank paper and a pencil for each participant

- Stopwatch or clock with second hand

• •

PROCESS

1. Prior to the session, prepare one container of twenty-five items for each subgroup and close the container.

2. Introduce the session by asking participants why they think it is important for service providers to be able to make accurate observations. After obtaining several responses, tell the participants that they will now have the opportunity to test their own observational skills.

3. Form subgroups of three to five persons each.

4. Distribute one container to each subgroup and one sheet of blank paper and a pencil to each participant.

5. Tell the subgroups that when you signal, they are to remove the lids from their containers and visually observe the contents for 10 seconds without speaking. Participants are not able to touch the objects during this time.

6. Time the task for exactly 10 seconds and then instruct the subgroups to replace the lids on their containers.

7. Tell individuals to make a list of the items they observed, without speaking to other group members. Allow a few minutes for completion of the task.

8. Tell the subgroups that they now will work together as a team to make a comprehensive listing of all the items they observed. Allow approximately 5 minutes for completion of the task, and then ask the groups to stop.

9. Direct the subgroups to open their containers and to compare the composite list against the items inside. Allow a few minutes for this task to be completed, and then ask each group in turn to report how many items were correctly identified.

10. Facilitate a large group discussion by asking the following questions:

   • How many items in the container was your group able to identify correctly?

   • Was this an improvement over your individual performance? Why or why not?

   • Were some items harder to remember than others? Why or why not?

   • Which items were most often remembered by the majority of the groups? Why do you think that was the case?

   • How much detail did you use in describing each item (for example, "red poker chip" rather than "poker chip")? Why?

   • What can individuals do to improve their observational skills in the workplace?

Conjecture Lecture

First Impressions

Goal To examine first impressions and their effect on how people relate to one another. Participants will make assumptions about personal characteristics of other group members based on brief job-related introductions.

Time Required Approximately 30 to 45 minutes

Group Size Subgroups of three or four persons each

Note This activity is intended for participants who have no prior knowledge of one another.

Materials

- One copy of the Conjecture Lecture Worksheet and a pencil for each participant
- Clock, timer, or stopwatch

• •

PROCESS

1. Form subgroups of three or four persons each. Direct the members of each group to count off to determine the order of participation in the activity.

2. Explain that each person will be introducing himself or herself to other members of the group by giving a 1-minute speech focusing on job skills as well as current and former positions. The beginning and ending times for each presentation will be announced.

3. Tell member 1 in each subgroup to begin and then call time after 1 minute. Repeat the process until all members of the groups have participated.

4. Explain that service providers often have only a few minutes of interaction with their customers, but in that short time, impressions can be formed on both sides. The participants now will use the introductory presentations as a basis for determining their personal perceptions of specific characteristics for each group member.

5. Distribute one copy of the worksheet and a pencil to each participant. Review the directions at the top of the sheet.

6. Allow approximately 5 minutes for completion of the task and then call time.

7. Ask the members of each group to discuss their responses and why they made them.

8. Allow approximately 10 minutes for small group discussion, giving a 1-minute warning before time expires.

9. Facilitate a large group discussion by asking the following questions:

   • Did your personal impressions differ from others in your group? How so?

   • In what ways do we create impressions of ourselves? How do these impressions affect the way in which others respond to us?

   • What are some examples of situations in which wrong impressions were made? What outcomes resulted?

   • What is the impact of personal filters and mental models on our actions with others?

   • How do personal filters and mental models influence stereotyping? What can be done to prevent stereotyping?

   • How can service representatives use first impressions to support the service provided to customers?

CONJECTURE LECTURE WORKSHEET

Directions: Record the names of the other members of your group in the spaces provided at the top of the table. Using your first impressions of each member in your group, place answers in the appropriate spaces for the listed characteristics.

TOPICS			
Marital status			
Children			
Pets			
Vehicle driven			
Hobbies			
Favorite color			

Information, Please

Observation and Information Gathering

Goal   To refine the skills of observation and information gathering. Participants will identify a preselected picture based on information provided by the facilitator.

Time Required   Approximately 30 minutes

Group Size   Five to fifteen participants

Materials

- Ten to twelve large pictures of similar content mounted on card stock

- Prize for winner (optional)

• •

PROCESS

1. Prior to the session, select ten to twelve large pictures that are similar in content (for example, landscape, house, room interior, individual, group of people) but that have some evident differences, and mount them on card stock. Display these pictures around the room so that all participants can see them.

2. Introduce the session by explaining that participants will be using information to determine which displayed picture is the one you selected to describe. Tell them that you will provide additional information only when someone requests "Information, please." Any time a guess is made and the picture is incorrect, that person is eliminated. You may choose to provide a prize to the winner to increase the motivation for participants to make a guess.

3. Mentally select one picture for which you will provide clues to the participants. Say, "I am thinking of a picture; which one is it?" As soon as someone requests, "Information, please," you then narrow the pictures down by stating one characteristic that eliminates at least one of the other pictures. (For example, if eight of the pictures have fences in them, you could say "a fence is visible," eliminating the other pictures.) Begin with broad information that eliminates only a few pictures so that participants continue to ask for more information as the game progresses.

4. Continue until a participant correctly guesses the selected picture. Provide a prize to the winner, if this option was chosen.

5. Facilitate a large group discussion by asking the following questions:

   • How well did you do in observing the subtle differences among the pictures?

   • Why are observation skills an important part of the customer service experience?

   • How did the information provided help you select a picture? How did it hinder the process?

   • Why are we sometimes reluctant to request additional information?

   • What are the implications of not having adequate information when making a decision?

   • How can this affect the way in which we meet customer needs?

It's a Jungle out There
Stereotyping

Goal   To explore how stereotypes can affect personal interactions. Participants will identify positive and negative traits for various jungle animals.

Time Required   Approximately 45 minutes

Group Size   Five subgroups of three to five persons each

Materials

● Pictures or figures of each of the following animals: giraffe, zebra, lion, elephant, gorilla

● Five newsprint sheets and a felt-tipped marker for the facilitator

● Masking tape for posting newsprint sheets

● One copy of the It's a Jungle out There Worksheet and a pencil for each person

PROCESS

1. Prior to the session, obtain the animal pictures or figures and place one each at five different tables or stations. Prepare one newsprint sheet with the name of each animal, and post.

2. As participants arrive, randomly assign each to one of the designated tables or stations.

3. Distribute a worksheet and a pencil to each person. Explain that each subgroup is to prepare a list of the traits, both positive and negative, that describe each of the five animals.

4. Allow approximately 15 minutes for group work, giving a 5-minute warning before time expires.

5. For each animal in turn, use a round-robin format to have the groups provide their lists of traits and record the words and phrases on the appropriate newsprint sheet.

6. Facilitate a large group discussion by asking the following questions:

    -   For those groups whose animals were described by others, how closely did the traits match your own list?

    -   How can we relate this exercise to stereotyping people?

    -   How are stereotypes formed?

    -   What stereotypical assumptions do we make about people?

    -   How do these assumptions affect our expectations of customers?

    -   How can service providers refrain from applying stereotypes?

VARIATION

After preparing the list of traits, have each subgroup identify customer behaviors that might be suggested by its assigned animal picture.

IT'S A JUNGLE OUT THERE WORKSHEET

Directions: Using words or phrases, describe several traits or characteristics (positive and negative) of each animal shown below.

Animal	Traits or Characteristics

Just My Luck
Personal Perspective

Goal   To examine personal perspective and its impact on how one perceives things. Participants will interpret a philosophical saying and share their interpretations.

Time Required   Approximately 45 minutes to 1 hour

Group Size   Subgroups of four or five persons each

Materials

- One fortune slip, one copy of the Just My Luck Worksheet, and a pencil for each participant

● ●

PROCESS

1. Prior to the session, prepare one fortune slip for each participant by cutting the Just My Luck Fortune Slips sheet into separate strips. A different fortune should be given to each subgroup, but members of each subgroup should have slips from the same fortune.

2. Introduce the session by stating that the way in which we interpret information and concepts shapes our perception of the world. Participants will have the opportunity to compare their personal perspectives with one another by interpreting some "bits of advice" that might be found in fortune cookies.

3. Form subgroups of four or five persons each.

4. Distribute one fortune slip, one worksheet, and a pencil to each participant.

5. Referring to the worksheet, review the directions and then tell the participants to work individually to complete the sheet.

6. Allow approximately 5 minutes for completion of the task, then ask members of each subgroup to discuss their individual interpretations and examples.

7. Allow approximately 15 minutes for group discussion, giving a 2-minute warning before time expires. Have a member of each subgroup read the fortune slip that was received, and ask for a review of the various interpretations and some examples that were provided.

8. Facilitate a large group discussion by asking the following questions:

   • How closely did your personal interpretation match those of other members of your group?

   • What were some of the similarities? Some differences?

   • Given that perception has a strong impact on the description and diagnosis of events, were the examples provided by the various group members more often similar or more often different? Be specific.

   • What factors contribute to how an individual perceives things? (*Answers might include culture, education, experience, upbringing, and so forth.*)

   • How does individual perception play a role in customer service interactions?

   • How can we use this information to improve the customer service experience?

JUST MY LUCK FORTUNE SLIPS

The doors to opportunity are marked push and pull.

Furious activity is no substitute for understanding.

The first time it is a favor; the second time a rule.

The road to success is always under construction.

It is a great piece of skill to know how to guide your luck, even while waiting for it.

Even the smallest candle burns brighter in the dark.

Mediocrity finds safety in standardization.

There are many paths to the top of the mountain, but the view is always the same.

The attacker must vanquish; the defender need only survive.

Men in the game are blind to what men looking on see clearly.

An ant may well destroy a whole dam.

JUST MY LUCK WORKSHEET

Directions: Take a few minutes to reflect on the philosophical saying written on the fortune slip you received. Next, write your interpretation of what the saying means to you. Finally, provide three examples of how this saying relates to actions that occur in your workplace.

Interpretation

Examples

1.

2.

3.

Making Sense of It
Sensory Acuity

Goal
To increase awareness of subtle physical cues through heightened sensory acuity. Participants will make observations of bodily reactions based on true or false responses to questions.

Time Required
Approximately 20 to 30 minutes

Group Size
Any number of pairs

Materials

- One copy of the Making Sense of It Instruction Sheet for each pair of participants

● ●

PROCESS

1. Introduce the session by stating that sensory acuity can increase awareness of the subtle nuances in physical reactions that occur as we interact with others.

2. Instruct the participants to form pairs. Ask the pairs to introduce themselves and provide some basic personal information—for example, where they were born, marital status, children, pets, and so forth.

3. Distribute one copy of the instruction sheet to one member of each pair and ask them to read the instructions to Part A.

4. Tell the pairs to begin. Allow approximately 5 minutes for the partners to complete Part A of the instructions.

5. Ask the partner with the instruction sheet to read Part B and then have the pairs begin the task.

6. Allow approximately 5 minutes for the partners to complete Part B and then ask them to stop.

7. Facilitate a discussion with the large group by asking the following questions:

    • For questioners, what were some of the physical changes you observed in your partner when he or she was not completely truthful?

    • How well did the questioner do in predicting the accuracy of the responses in Part B? Why?

    • Why is it necessary to look for *patterns* of behavior when using your observational skills? *(If you use isolated incidents or reactions, you can misjudge actions or people.)*

    • How can awareness of the external body language of others help in our interactions with customers? *(Empathize when others are upset, probe for more information if you feel there is more information needed, handle anger.)*

MAKING SENSE OF IT INSTRUCTION SHEET

You will be asking your partner a series of questions. Your task is to watch the changes in facial expression, body posture, and breathing as your partner answers your questions.

Notice and remember all the unconscious visible responses to the YES questions and compare them to those for the NO questions. Be aware of the differences in breathing, skin color, and lower lip, and any minute muscle movements of the face.

Part A

1. Tell your partner that you will be asking a series of questions and that he or she is to honestly answer yes or no.

2. Referring to the introductory personal information you received from your partner, ask three questions you know will be answered yes. *(For example, if your partner stated that he owned a dog, you ask if he had a pet.)* Then ask three questions you know will be answered no. *(For example, if your partner stated that she was married, you ask if she is single.)*

3. Continue to alternate YES and NO questions until you feel confident that you recognize the difference in your partner's responses.

Part B

1. Tell your partner that you will be asking a series of YES or NO questions again and that he or she can choose to answer truthfully or not.

2. Ask a series of obscure questions to which you do not know the answers. For example,

   - Did you wear your hair long when you were a teenager?

   - Is your mother older than your father?

   - Did you ever own a motorcycle?

   - Would you like to visit Egypt?

After each question, try to guess whether the answer is true or not by using your "extra" sensory perception. Check the accuracy of your prediction with your partner.

See Saw

Visual Perception

Goal
To discover the relationship between what is seen and what is perceived. Participants will identify objects based on verbal descriptions.

Time Required
Approximately 30 to 45 minutes

Group Size
Eight to twenty participants

Materials

- One sheet of blank paper and a pencil for each participant

- Eight to ten common objects (for example, stapler, stuffed animal, plant, globe)

● ●

PROCESS

1. Prior to the session, place half of the objects in a front corner of the room and half in a back corner. These objects are in addition to other items normally found in the room.

2. Distribute one blank sheet of paper and a pencil to each participant.

3. Direct all participants to face the front of the room. Ask for a volunteer.

4. Explain that the participants will be trying to identify specific objects that will be described by the volunteer. The name of each object is to be written on the paper provided, numbered sequentially.

5. Tell the volunteer to look at the front corner of the room where you placed the additional objects (define the limits of the "corner") and describe everything that he or she sees there, *without naming any of the actual objects, their composition materials, or their uses.* The descriptions should be in terms of line, shape, color, texture, size, apparent weight, translucence, and so forth. *(For example, a vase could be described as slender, green, and ten inches tall, but* not *as glass or as a container to hold flowers. This description also mistakenly might lead a participant to select a plant as the object being described.)* Tell the volunteer to record each object in sequential order after describing it.

6. After the volunteer finishes the descriptions, ask participants to name the objects. The volunteer will verify the answers against his or her master list.

7. Tell the participants to turn their sheets over and to use the back of the sheet for the next set of descriptions.

8. Ask for another volunteer to repeat the exercise, but now ask for descriptions of objects that are found in the back corner of the room in which you placed the additional objects. The rest of the participants are to remain facing forward, again trying to identify the objects described.

9. After the volunteer finishes these descriptions, ask the participants to name the objects and have the volunteer verify the answers.

10. Facilitate a large group discussion by asking the following questions:

    • How well did you do in identifying the objects in the front of the room?

    • What helped or hindered the identification process? *(help: seeing objects, numerous descriptors; hinder: not enough information, vague descriptions, objects too much alike)*

- How well did you do in identifying the objects in the back of the room? Why? *(Could not see objects, didn't know use.)*

- How do visual cues help us "read" a situation? *(individual features, facial expressions, body language, environment, examining things within the context of the situation)* How do they hinder us? *(Too much similarity can lead to assumptions and stereotyping.)*

- How does perception of a situation influence interactions and outcomes?

- In relation to the concept of perception, what can you do to improve customer interactions?

Stressing the Positive
Workplace Stressors

Goal
To reduce workplace stress factors. The participants will identify causes of work stress and develop possible solutions.

Time Required
Approximately 1 to 1½ hours

Group Size
Three to five subgroups of no more than six persons each

Materials

- One copy of the Stressing the Positive Checklist and a pencil for each participant

- One copy of the Stressing the Positive Worksheet, one newsprint sheet, and a felt-tipped marker for each subgroup

- Flip chart and felt-tipped marker for recording information

- Masking tape for posting newsprint sheets

• •

PROCESS

1. Introduce the session by explaining that certain organizational factors can contribute to high stress levels. A certain amount of stress keeps us from experiencing "rust-out," whereby too few demands cause a lack of motivation. However, excessive or continuous stress can cause "burnout," emotional and physical exhaustion that affects both our health and our work. Explain that participants will be identifying the sources of stress as the first step in learning how to deal with it.

2. Distribute one copy of the checklist and a pencil to each participant. Direct individuals to identify the things that they feel raise workplace stress levels.

3. Allow several minutes for task completion and then collect the checklists. Tally the number of responses to each item and record the top three to five items on a flip chart.

4. Use the list to lead a general discussion on each of the items with such questions as:

   - Why does this happen?

   - Is the factor that causes this stress within your control?

   - What can your service team do to correct the situation?

   - Who can you get to help with this situation?

5. Form three to five subgroups of no more than six persons each (depending on the number of stress factors listed) and assign one of the stressors to each subgroup.

6. Distribute one worksheet, one newsprint sheet, and a felt-tipped marker to each subgroup.

7. Direct the subgroups to complete the worksheet using the assigned stress factor. Then, using the newsprint sheet, the group should list at least three suggestions for reducing the stress factor. Each group should be prepared to present a full explanation of each idea.

8. Allow approximately 30 minutes for group work, giving a 5-minute warning before time expires.

9. Provide masking tape and ask the subgroups to post the newsprint sheets. Ask each subgroup in turn to report the background information from the worksheet and the three suggestions that were developed.

STRESSING THE POSITIVE CHECKLIST

Directions: Check off all the factors that you feel contribute to excessive stress in the workplace.

- ☐ Workload too heavy
- ☐ Time pressures
- ☐ Constantly changing priorities
- ☐ Lack of direction
- ☐ Too much direction
- ☐ Lack of performance feedback
- ☐ Lack of information
- ☐ Too much information
- ☐ Demands for higher productivity
- ☐ Demands for improved quality
- ☐ Meetings
- ☐ Interruptions
- ☐ Budget cuts
- ☐ Lack of staff
- ☐ Incompetent or unmotivated people
- ☐ Uncertainty of job security
- ☐ Strict policies and procedures

STRESSING THE POSITIVE WORKSHEET

Stress Factor:

Causes:

Possible Solutions:

Suggested Action Plan:

Resources Needed:

Possible Consequences:

What Now?

Perceptual Expectations

Goal   To explore how individual perception influences expected outcomes and results. Participants will create endings to prescribed situations.

Time Required   Approximately 45 minutes

Group Size   Subgroups of three to five persons each

Materials

- One copy of the What Now? Worksheet and a pencil for each participant

● ●

PROCESS

1. Introduce the session by stating that the individual perception of events can influence the expected outcomes or results of various situations.

2. Ask the following question and facilitate a group discussion:

    •   What factors affect the way in which we view the world? *(personal values, education, religious beliefs, family upbringing, economic status, personality, maturity level, relationships with others, emotional state, current events)*

    Explain that this unique view of the world characterizes an individual's perception. The way in which we perceive things and events, in turn, influences how we make observations and anticipate or judge outcomes. A simplified example of this is for one person who sees someone running down the street to assume that she is running toward something (catching a bus) and another person to assume that the individual is running away from something (fleeing a robbery).

3. Explain that the participants will have the opportunity to examine their own perceptions of events and then compare them with those of other participants.

4. Distribute one copy of the worksheet and a pencil to each participant. Direct the participants to complete the sheet by creating endings for the situations given.

5. Allow approximately 10 minutes for completion of the task, giving a 2-minute warning before time expires.

6. Form subgroups of three to five persons each. Ask members of the subgroups to discuss their endings for the situations.

7. Allow approximately 10 minutes for discussion, then ask for examples of endings for each situation in turn.

8. Facilitate a large group discussion by asking the following questions:

    •   How closely did individual endings compare to those of other group members?

    •   What are some examples of similarities? Differences?

    •   How do expected outcomes influence customer service interactions?

    •   What are some actions that can be taken to align both customer and service provider expectations?

WHAT NOW? WORKSHEET

Directions: Write an ending for each situation presented below.

1. An express train is rolling rapidly along the tracks as a large brown cow lumbers up onto the rails. *What happens next?*

2. Pat Peters is driving an old car and steers onto a one-way street in the wrong direction. *What happens next?*

3. Kim and Casey are in the supermarket shopping for watermelons. They both arrive at the bin at the same instant. Only one watermelon is sitting in the bin. *What happens next?*

4. A cat discovers a fishbowl with one big fish in it. With whiskers twitching and nose to the glass, the cat follows the fish swimming around and around in the bowl. Unknown to the cat, the fish is a meat-eating piranha. *What happens next?*

5. Alex and Sydney are carrying their dishes on trays in the cafeteria line. Alex stops abruptly. *What happens next?*

On the Line

Credibility

Customers expect reliability and trustworthiness from their service providers. To be credible in the eyes of customers, employees must provide accurate information, be accountable for their actions, and value the customer as an individual. Customers will remain true to the company when its service representatives perform consistently, practice discretion, and commit to a respectful relationship with them.

Directions: How credible do you feel you are in the eyes of your customers? Think about your daily actions and then circle either YES or NO for each of the following statements to help you identify your individual strengths and weaknesses.

1. I treat all customers with respect and care.   YES   NO

2. I am fully knowledgeable about my company's products and services.   YES   NO

3. If I can't answer questions immediately, I know where to find the answers.   YES   NO

4. I never make light of a customer's concern or complaint.   YES   NO

5. I always give a positive and empathetic response to customer complaints.   YES   NO

6. I use polite and courteous language around customers.   YES   NO

7. I never divulge details of my customer's transactions to others.   YES   NO

8. I admit my mistakes and offer to make things right.   YES   NO

9. I consistently follow through when I promise to call a customer back.   YES   NO

10. I provide extra information about products and services without
being asked.   YES   NO

11. When I can't give the customer exactly what he or she wants, I provide alternatives.   YES   NO

12. I don't place blame for customer problems on any individual or
department.   YES   NO

13. I don't criticize the behavior of coworkers.   YES   NO

14. I don't complain about my boss, management, or working
conditions.   YES   NO

15. I treat all my customers equally and fairly.   YES   NO

Scoring: How did you rate? If you responded YES to 12 or more of the statements, you already are doing much of what it takes to gain the trust and respect of your customers. Examine the areas that still need improvement and reflect on those situations where your credibility failed to shine.

Now jot down some possible work issues that may be contributing to reduced credibility with your customers.

Work Issues That Hinder Credibility

To the Facilitator   After completion of the questionnaires, form small groups to discuss some of the work issues identified by individuals. Conduct a large group discussion regarding the ratings and then use feedback from the subgroups to list the issues on a flip chart. Identify those areas that might be improved and list specific actions that can be taken, along with timelines.

Power Up
Assertiveness

Do you feel that others take advantage of you? Or are you aggressive, meeting your own needs at the expense of others? Do you think you express your thoughts, feelings, and beliefs in a direct, honest, and appropriate way? An assertive person effectively influences, listens, and negotiates so that others choose to cooperate willingly. Being assertive is one of the most important skills you can have. In your daily work communication, you need to be assertive when handling complaints, selling, negotiating, motivating, or delegating.

Directions: Consider the following statements and check the answer that describes your behavior in MOST situations.

		YES	NO
1.	Others find it easy to take advantage of me.	____	____
2.	I hesitate to speak up for fear others might consider me aggressive.	____	____
3.	I sound as though I am asking a question when I am making a statement.	____	____
4.	I preface my comments with disclaimers such as "I may be wrong" or "This might be a stupid question, but . . ."	____	____

	YES	NO
5. I say too much and give too many details when I explain something.	____	____
6. I accept what I'm offered even when it's not what I wanted or expected.	____	____
7. I avoid saying things I feel in order to keep the peace.	____	____
8. I downplay compliments when I receive them.	____	____
9. I allow myself to be pressured into making snap decisions.	____	____
10. I say yes when I want to say no.	____	____
11. I feel the need to invent excuses when I say no.	____	____
12. I remain silent when criticized or treated unfairly.	____	____
13. I allow myself to be inconvenienced in order to avoid conflicts.	____	____
14. I feel guilty when I say no.	____	____
15. I talk around the issue rather than express my feelings directly.	____	____
16. I make promises I later regret.	____	____
17. I respond impetuously rather than carefully choose my words.	____	____
18. I get angry at myself when I choose not to say things I should have said.	____	____
19. I respond defensively when unfairly criticized.	____	____
20. I lose my courage at the last moment and don't say what I planned to say when I am faced with an awkward or threatening situation.	____	____

Total of YES responses: _____

Scoring:

15–19 You are too timid.

7–14 You should be more assertive.

0–6 You are self-assured.

Assertiveness Tips

- Use "I" rather than "you" messages.

- Express feelings and needs without blame or punishment.

- Resolve issues immediately.

- Learn to say no without guilt.

- Keep control by speaking in a firm voice and maintaining a well-balanced posture.

- Focus objectively on the situation and do not get sidetracked.

- Express your case with conviction, but don't neglect the position of the other person.

Personal Improvement Goals:

_____

_____

_____

_____

_____

To the Facilitator   After completion of the rating forms, form small groups to discuss some of the goals identified by individuals and issues that hinder assertive behavior. Conduct a large group discussion regarding specific actions that can be taken to improve assertive behaviors that meet the needs of the customer (internal and external) as well as those of the service representative.

Flex Your Mind
Mental Flexibility

Individual

Flexibility in mental responses means changing old patterns and ways of responding. When you break out of your old rut of routine stimulus-response, you can discover new talents, propensities, and ways of communicating. Opening your mind to more and varied possibilities will help you solve customer problems in unique ways. In order to improve mental flexibility, however, you need to practice.

● ●

ACTIONS

- Interrupt old patterns by driving to work using a different route.

- Look at the world through a new set of eyeglasses—pretend you are 12 or 92 years old.

- Do something you have never done before: write a poem or learn to knit.

- Solve puzzles that involve lateral and critical thinking.

- In low-risk situations, stop what you are doing and think of three alternative ways to reach the proposed outcome.

- Switch from your primary sense of perception to another mode. For example, if you rely on visual cues, try tuning to sounds or feelings.

- Switch the sequences of information you use when making a decision.

- Make a list of all your habits for a week; then, on the following week, change the time of day you do each habitual activity or do some of them in different sequences.

Keep It Cool
Job Pressure

Individual

No matter where you work, you probably find times when you think nothing can go right. When things start to "heat up" and the pressures of the job are getting you down, think of ways to keep cool under pressure. Here are a few ideas to get you started.

● ●

ACTIONS

- Take three slow, deep, relaxing breaths to clear your mind and calm your thoughts.

- Look for the amusing side of a difficult situation.

- Post motivational quotes near your desk.

- Keep a funny picture or comics feature near your phone so that you remember to smile.

- Take a brisk walk during your break time.

- Take breaks with coworkers who are fun to be with.

- Throw yourself a 5-minute party with a treat from home.

- Turn on some music, get up from your chair, and dance a little.

- Pair up with one or more colleagues and send humorous e-cards to one another.

- Review your successes at the end of the day.

Stress Buster
Stress Reduction

Leader

Stress can be a very real barrier to effective job performance. In the customer service field, stress can be a constant companion as employees deal with such things as information overload, customer demands, and service complaints. It is important to recognize when your staff has reached the "boiling point" and to take the time for a little R & R (recovery and refocus).

● ●

ACTION

Create a stress tolerance thermometer:

1. Draw a big thermometer on a poster board and mark approximately thirty lines along the length of the thermometer. Display the chart in a space accessible to all group members.

2. Explain to employees that by gauging the team's stress level, the thermometer will help keep the group from becoming "stressed out."

3. Give each employee ten red dots and encourage them to place a dot on the thermometer whenever they feel overly stressed. Ask them to write what the stressor is next to the red dot.

4. When the red dots start to bubble off the chart, have a stress reduction party.

5. Use the causes listed on the chart to facilitate a discussion with the group about how to reduce the causes of the stress.

Meltdown
Dealing with Anger

When confronted with an angry person, you first have to accept that anger is a legitimate emotion—one that many of us find difficult to express appropriately. Therefore, when a person does express anger, you must assume that there is a valid reason for it. You also should recognize that some people are more volatile than others, some have less self-control, and some respond more to "gut reaction" than to logic. Here are some guidelines for managing an angry customer:

- Respond with a firm approach and a direct facial expression. Maintain a calm and composed stance throughout the encounter.

- Attract the customer's attention by saying his or her name, if possible. Keeping eye contact, follow through immediately with a short statement, showing you recognize and acknowledge the anger: "You are obviously very annoyed; what exactly went wrong?"

- Empathize, acknowledging the customer's point of view. It is important that you don't imply that the company is a mess or that the staff is incompetent. Professionalism and loyalty to the organization must be paramount.

- Establish the facts of the situation while keeping a calm, even tone and level of voice.

- If appropriate, apologize once and sincerely for the inconvenience caused by any error or misunderstanding, then set about putting things right.

- Repeat your statement of intent until the customer calms down. It may be possible to offer an alternative: "Would you like to speak to the manager?"

- Ask if anything further can be done to improve things and, if the person has any suggestions, use active listening to check facts. Affirm that you have heard and understood.

- If the situation gets out of control, call for a manager or offer to have someone call the customer back. Remember that you have the right to be treated with respect and not to be threatened.

Things to Do

- Stay calm.

- Maintain a neutral posture, facial expression, and tone of voice. Keep steady eye contact.

- Allow the other person some time to "let off steam."

- Acknowledge the person's anger and empathize, as appropriate.

- Listen well and let the other person know that you heard and understood what was said.

- Try to establish the cause of the anger and do what you can to establish a solution, a workable relationship, a compromise, or some other positive outcome.

- Help the other person behave assertively, rather than aggressively, by your example.

Things to Avoid

- Don't show impatience or annoyance.

- Don't let the customer dominate the conversation; gently intervene by restating what was said and then move the conversation along.

- Don't get sidetracked by other issues.

- Don't cut off the other person's speech too abruptly; treat the situation with care and sensitivity.

- Don't overdo your apology or place blame on other employees and the organization.

Plead Your Case
Influencing Change

In psychological terms, *set* describes a person's tendency to see things in a certain way, to do things in a certain way, and to stick to the familiar because it's more comfortable than changing. A person's psychological set determines his or her subjective interpretation of an external situation. In order to get others to change their sets and accept what you are offering in terms of service or products, you may need to incorporate a bit of persuasion. Such influence helps get people to *want* to do what you propose them to do.

Facts to Remember

- You need to understand the other person's set—do not challenge it.

- Arguing will not change someone's set, only threaten it, which will cause the other individual to dig in harder.

- If you stay mired in your own set, you will get nowhere in moving toward change.

- If you can see things the way the other person sees them, you have a chance to build trust and change his or her set.

- If others show resistance to your attempts at persuasion, determine which of the following causes may be to blame. This may help you change their sets.

Possible Causes of Resistance:

- Not readily forsaking the old for the new and untried

- Not breaking established habits unless absolutely required to

- Not taking initiative easily if doing so can be avoided

- Not sacrificing present security for possible future advantage

- Not acting on anything unless prodded

- Not giving up prejudices easily

- Not openly admitting ignorance or incompetence

- Not trusting the new information or the person representing it

Remedies:

- *Alignment.* What you propose must be consistent with your past words and actions.

- *Association.* Connect what is already accepted with what you want to be accepted. Connect people with their needs and wants.

- *Confidence.* If you are confident, then others can be confident.

- *Evidence.* People cannot deny what they see with their own eyes.

- *Framing.* Meaning depends on context, so give broad details about other contributory factors before making your major point, and reframe others' objections into benefits.

- *Logic.* Understand the real logic of both your and others' arguments within the social and emotional situation.

- *Objectivity.* Stand back to decrease emotion and increase rational, logical thinking.

- *Perception.* Work from what people believe by fitting what you say into their mental models and by using their language.

- *Trust.* If you are trustworthy, people will be more likely to accept what you have to say.

Communication

ood customer service relies on effective communication as a means of gathering necessary details, providing information, and responding to customer concerns. This means that the service interaction must be built on clear, concise, and accurate communication skills. The service provider and the customer must listen to one another and must speak in a way the other party can understand. This means that the service representative must facilitate the interaction in ways that help customers give and receive information more effectively.

Successful communication helps avoid misunderstandings and creates a positive impression with customers. It requires that service representatives be able to put things in proper perspective by interpreting the information within the context of the specific situation. In order to do this, they must recognize that each customer is unique in his or her beliefs and feelings and that circumstances affect the meaning of communication. This interpretation occurs through both verbal and nonverbal expressions.

Verbal communication is a two-way process involving both a sender and a receiver. It involves expressing thoughts clearly, accurately, completely, and concisely; listening or reading attentively; and asking questions when necessary. Language must be clear and consistent, and details must be complete and concise so that the message comes through as intended. This requires a dialogue between customer and service provider, and questioning is a critical component of effective two-way communication.

Often the only connection with a valuable customer is the telephone. The service provider must combat the depersonalization of phone communications to be as effective as he or she would be in a face-to-face interaction. Listening is not a passive activity, but a skill that requires concentration and practice. A service representative's active, responsive listening can surmount a tense situation and build good rapport with customers and associates alike.

Communication experts estimate that in face-to-face interactions, almost 90 percent of the meaning of the message is conveyed through nonverbal communication. "Body language" (body movements, gestures, posture, eye movements, facial expressions, and so forth) and voice qualities can detract from or enhance the communication process. How one perceives and interprets these nonverbal cues depends to a large degree on personal experiences, expectations, emotional state, and knowledge of others. Whether intentional or unintentional, body language provides clues about the sender and may guide the outcome of the interaction either positively or negatively.

Gaining a better understanding of the many ways in which words, vocal qualities, and gestures can be interpreted is critical to an individual's ability to perceive and react to changing environments. Competing within a global economy, service providers must interact with customers in an increasingly multicultural environment. They will be required to use highly effective communication skills to support and sustain their organization's ability to meet the needs of diverse populations, both nationally and internationally.

Blueprints for Success
Verbal Instructions

Goal   To practice giving and receiving verbal instructions. Participants will follow a series of verbal instructions to assemble a construction from toy pieces.

Time Required   Approximately 30 to 45 minutes

Group Size   Five to fifteen participants

Materials

- One plastic bag and closure for each participant

- Twenty to thirty Lego® pieces (of varied shapes, colors, and sizes) for each partici-pant (*Note:* All sets must be identical.)

- One assembled construction

- Medium-size box

● ●

PROCESS

1. Prior to the session, prepare an identical construction set for each participant by inserting twenty to thirty Lego pieces into a plastic bag and then closing it. Next, assemble a unit using all the pieces from one of the construction sets. Place the construction inside the box so that the open section of the box is oriented to the side, making the construction visible from that end.

2. At the session, ask for a volunteer to provide verbal instructions for the rest of the participants to follow. Taking the person aside, present the box with the construction inside and direct the volunteer to keep the assembly hidden from the rest of the group while instructions are being given.

3. Distribute one construction set to each remaining participant.

4. Explain that the volunteer will be giving an oral description of the pieces and steps to follow in assembling a construction that is identical to the one in the box. Do not make reference to the participants' ability to ask questions, but if questions are asked, they are allowed.

5. Direct the volunteer to begin.

6. After the construction has been fully described by the volunteer and reproduced by the participants, stop the activity and have the volunteer reveal the construction from inside the box. Ask the participants to compare their individual constructions against the model.

7. Facilitate a large group discussion by asking the following questions:

   - How did you feel while the instructions were being given? Why do you think these reactions occurred?

   - How closely did the individual constructions fit the model? What factors contributed to this?

   - What could have been described better?

   - If people asked questions, in what way did the questions help clarify information? If no one asked questions, why did you choose to refrain from doing so?

   - How does this activity relate to giving and receiving information during the customer service experience?

   - What actions can we take to improve our ability to give instructions? To receive instructions?

From Me to You

Focus on Others

Goal
To focus on others during the communication process. Participants will try to use the word "you" more than the word "I" while speaking for specified periods of time.

Time Required
Approximately 15 to 20 minutes

Group Size
Subgroups of three persons each

Materials

- One sheet of blank paper and a pencil for each participant

- Stopwatch or clock with a second hand

PROCESS

1. Begin the activity by saying that it is often difficult for us to move away from our self-interest when we interact or communicate with others. Explain that the participants will have an opportunity to practice focusing on others in a more conscious way.

2. Form subgroups of three persons each. Ask members of each group to count off as 1, 2, or 3.

3. Distribute one sheet of blank paper and a pencil to each participant. Ask the participants to make two columns on the paper and mark one column I and the other one You.

4. Explain that person 3 will be speaking to person 2 for 30 seconds about anything he or she would like to discuss. (Some suggested topics might be best vacation spots, favorite music, pets, hobbies, and so forth.) The object is to try to use the word "you" as much as possible and avoid using the word "I." Person 1 will keep count of the number of times each word is used and record these by placing a check in the appropriate column on the paper.

5. Announce for groups to begin and time the task for 30 seconds. Stop the groups when time expires. Tell the recorders to turn their papers over until later.

6. Explain that person 2 will be speaking to person 1 for 1 minute about anything he or she would like to discuss while trying to use the word "you" as much as possible and avoiding the word "I." Person 3 will keep count of the number of times each word is used and record these on the paper.

7. Announce for groups to begin and time the task for 1 minute. Stop the groups when time expires. Tell the recorders to turn their papers over until later.

8. Explain that person 1 will be speaking to person 3 for 2 minutes about anything he or she would like to discuss, using "you" as much as possible and avoiding the use of "I." Person 2 will keep count of the words and record them.

9. Announce for groups to begin and time the task for 2 minutes. Stop the groups when time expires.

10. Ask the recorders from each group to report the usage of the words, starting with the 30-second time period and ending with the 2-minute time period.

11. Facilitate a large group discussion by asking the following questions:

- How did you feel while you were the person talking?

- Was it more or less difficult to avoid saying "I" when the time period was extended? Why?

- How do you feel when talking or listening to someone who constantly uses the word "I"?

- How can we phrase our communications to better focus on the other person?

- How does this activity relate to customer service?

Negative Ten-dency
Word Usage

Goal
To examine the impact of specific words on the communication process. Participants will identify words that provoke a negative response for them.

Time Required
Approximately 30 to 45 minutes

Group Size
Subgroups of three to five persons each

Materials

- One copy of the Negative Ten-dency Worksheet and a pencil for each person

PROCESS

1. Explain to the participants that they will be examining how specific words can affect the interpretation of a message.

2. Distribute a copy of the worksheet and a pencil to each participant.

3. Direct each participant to write down ten words, excluding obscenities, that for them provoke strong negative responses. Allow approximately 5 minutes for individual work.

4. Form subgroups of three to five participants each.

5. Ask the groups to discuss the chosen words and the reasons why they were chosen. Allow approximately 10 minutes for small group discussion.

6. Facilitate a large group discussion based on the following questions:

   • What "types" of words were selected?

   • Are there similarities among the words that were chosen? What were they?

   • What events or experiences led to the negative meaning of the words?

   • When we communicate with others, what assumptions might occur as a result of our word choices?

   • What role does perception (our personal view of the world) play in this process?

   • How does a negative response during the communication process affect the outcome of an interaction? How does it affect conflict resolution, specifically?

   • How can we use this information to communicate better with customers?

NEGATIVE TEN-DENCY WORKSHEET

Directions: List ten words that you feel provoke a strong negative response from you.

1. _____

2. _____

3. _____

4. _____

5. _____

6. _____

7. _____

8. _____

9. _____

10. _____

Poker Face
Nonverbal Communication

Goal   To examine nonverbal communication in terms of feelings and reactions. Participants will play a game of poker while others observe the actions of the players.

Time Required   Approximately 45 minutes

Group Size   An even number of subgroups with three to five persons each

Materials

- One deck of playing cards and poker chips for one-half of the total number of subgroups

- One Poker Face Role Card for each member of the Player subgroups (approximately one-half of participants)

- One Poker Face Hand Rankings Sheet for each participant

- One sheet of blank paper and a pencil for each member of the Observer subgroups (approximately one-half of participants)

- One table for each Player subgroup

• •

PROCESS

1. Introduce the session by stating that poker is a game in which losing and winning can depend in large part on the ability of the player to "bluff" or to act out in a certain way. Participants will have the opportunity to examine the nonverbal communication cues that might occur in these situations.

2. Form an even number of subgroups with three to five persons each. Assign half of the subgroups to be Players and the other half to be Observers.

3. Situate each Player subgroup at a separate table with members of an Observer group surrounding each one.

4. Provide one deck of playing cards and poker chips to each Player subgroup. Distribute one sheet of paper and a pencil to each member of the Observer subgroups.

5. Distribute one copy of the hand rankings sheet to each card player and clarify any questions.

6. Assign one Poker Face Role Card to each player, with a warning to keep the cards hidden from others.

7. Explain that the members of the Player subgroups are to play several hands of some form of poker, making legitimate bets with the poker chips in an effort to win. Tell the players that they are to maintain the characteristic assigned to each throughout the entire game. The members of the Observer subgroups are to carefully study the nonverbal cues of the players and make notes on the sheet provided.

8. Signal for the poker games to start. Allow approximately 7 to 10 minutes and then stop the groups.

9. Ask the observers to report their findings, then ask the players to reveal their assigned characteristics.

10. Facilitate a large group discussion by asking the following questions:

    • For players, how did you feel about yourself in this situation? How did you feel about your opponents?

    • What nonverbal clues did you pick up as players? As observers?

    • Did these nonverbal actions seem congruent with the situation? Why or why not?

- What are some of the characteristics of the nonverbal actions given by particular players? What would these clues normally mean in real-life situations?

- For players, how did maintaining a "consistent expression" affect your playing? Why?

- In the workplace, what are some situations in which we sometimes win by concealing the truth and projecting useful falsehoods?

- How do nonverbal communication cues affect how we interact with others? What impact does this have on situational outcomes?

POKER FACE ROLE CARDS

ANGRY	TRIUMPHANT
DISHEARTENED	CONFIDENT
ANNOYED	SELF-IMPORTANT
DISMAYED	BORED
DISAPPOINTED	ANXIOUS
SUSPICIOUS	NERVOUS

POKER FACE HAND RANKINGS SHEET

The following poker hands are ranked from highest to lowest. If there are two or more hands that qualify, the one with the higher-ranking cards wins.

Royal flush: A straight from a ten to an ace and all five cards of the same suit. In poker, suit does not matter; pots are split between equally strong hands.

Straight flush: Any straight with all five cards of the same suit.

Four of a kind: Any four cards of the same rank. If two players share the same four of a kind, the fifth card will decide who wins the pot—the higher card wins.

Full house: Any three cards of the same rank together with any two cards of the same rank. Ties are broken first by the three of a kind, then the pair.

Flush: Any five cards of the same suit that are not consecutive. The highest card of the five determines the rank of the flush.

Straight: Any five consecutive cards of different suits. The ace counts as either a high or a low card.

Three of a kind: Any three cards of the same rank.

Two pair: Any two cards of the same rank together with another two cards of the same rank. The higher pair of the two determines the rank of the two pair.

One pair: Any two cards of the same rank.

High card: Any hand that does not make up any of the above-mentioned hands.

Say What You Mean
Concise Verbal Communication

Goal   To focus on the importance of clear and concise verbal communication. Participants will follow verbal instructions for writing the numeral 5.

Time Required   Approximately 30 minutes

Group Size   Six to thirty participants

Materials

- Two sheets of blank paper and a pencil for each participant

- One copy of the Say What You Mean Instruction Sheet for the facilitator

- One sheet of blank paper and a felt-tipped marker for the facilitator

- Flip chart for recording

● ●

PROCESS

1. Prior to the session, use a felt-tipped marker to draw the numeral 5 on a sheet of paper by following Instruction Set B on the instruction sheet.

2. Introduce the session by stating that the ability to give and follow accurate verbal instructions is an important feature of meeting customer needs. This activity is designed to help the participants focus on the importance of clear oral communication.

3. Distribute two sheets of paper and a pencil to each participant.

4. Explain that the participants are to use one sheet of paper to draw the "secret object" as you describe it; no questions allowed. Using the instruction sheet, read aloud Instruction Set A, pausing after each step.

5. Direct the participants to hold up their completed pictures for everyone to view. Discuss the differences among the various drawings.

6. Without revealing the "real" picture or giving any hints, ask the following questions in turn. Record the answers on the flip chart:

    • What questions would you have liked to ask as the instructions were being given?

    • What words or phrases could have been used to help you draw the picture more accurately?

7. Direct the participants to use the other sheet of paper to follow your instructions again. Read aloud Instruction Set B, pausing after each step.

8. Direct the participants to hold up the new pictures for everyone to view. Show the participants your picture of the numeral 5 created prior to the session.

9. Discuss why the second set of pictures is more uniform than the first set. Ask for specific words and phrases that were "muddy" or "clear" and record these on appropriate flip-chart sheets.

10. Facilitate a large group discussion by asking the following questions:

    • Why is two-way communication so important?

    • In what types of service situation is clear verbal communication a vital aspect?

    • What are the possible results of unclear communication in these situations?

- What are some examples of real-world experiences where communication broke down and the resulting outcome was unfavorable?

- What specific steps can employees take to make the communication process clear and effective?

SAY WHAT YOU MEAN INSTRUCTION SHEET

Instruction Set A

1. Draw a short line.

2. Draw another line touching the first line you drew.

3. Put your pen at the other end of the second line and draw a half circle.

Instruction Set B

1. Starting in the middle of your paper, draw a horizontal line about 1 inch long.

2. Place the point of your pencil on the place where the horizontal line begins, on the left. From that point, draw a vertical line that extends approximately 1 inch.

3. Starting where the second line ends, draw a backwards **C**, going from top to bottom. The tips of the backwards **C** should be about 1 inch apart.

Seeing Is Believing
Body Language and Culture

Goal   To explore how body language conveys meaning that is subject to cultural interpretations. Participants will create defined gestures and test their interpretations at an "international meeting."

Time Required   Approximately 1 hour

Group Size   Subgroups of three to five persons each, with a maximum of thirty participants

Materials

● Two sheets of paper and a pencil for each subgroup

• •

PROCESS

1. Introduce the session by stating that recognizing cultural gestures has become vital as business has become global. Participants will have the opportunity to explore body language as a means of communication.

2. Demonstrate the following gestures, asking the participants for some general comments on their interpretations of each one:

    A. Nod your head up and down (yes).

    B. Point at something with your index finger.

    C. Pass something with one hand.

    D. Wave your hand back and forth with palm facing outward (greet someone).

3. Explain that common gestures such as these mean different things in different cultures. For example, in most places nodding your head up and down (A) signifies yes, but it means no in parts of Greece, Bulgaria, and Turkey. Using your index finger to point (B) is impolite in the Middle and Far East, and passing something with one hand (C) is very rude in Japan. Rather than a friendly greeting in many places, waving your hand back and forth (D) means no in Europe.

4. Form subgroups of three to five persons each. Ask each group to select a member to record information.

5. Distribute two sheets of paper and a pencil to each subgroup.

6. Tell participants that each subgroup will have 10 minutes in which to create some unique gestures and describe their meanings on the paper provided.

7. Allow approximately 10 minutes for task completion, giving a 2-minute warning before time expires.

8. Explain that the entire group will participate in an "international meeting" where each person will use the new gestures created by his or her subgroup to communicate with members of other groups. Verbal language may accompany the body language, but it should not directly relay the meaning of the gestures being used. Participants will try to discover the meaning of the gestures created by other subgroups as they interact with one another. Direct the participants to move about and intermingle.

9. Allow approximately 15 minutes for interaction and then call time. Ask participants to return to their appropriate subgroups.

10. Have members of each subgroup in turn demonstrate the gestures they created. Get feedback on the meaning of each gesture from other groups before having the originating group describe its meaning.

11. Facilitate a large group discussion by asking the following questions:

    • Personally, how did you feel while you were interacting with others during the "meeting"?

    • How difficult was it to interpret the various gestures? Why?

    • What hindered the process? What helped?

    • How does the perception of body language influence customer service interactions?

    • What can a service provider do to gain a better understanding of an increasingly multicultural service environment?

Summary Judgment
Listening

Goal   To improve listening effectiveness. Participants will paraphrase or summarize prior information before entering a conversation.

Time Required   Approximately 30 minutes

Group Size   Subgroups of five or six persons each

Materials

- None

PROCESS

1. Form subgroups of five or six persons each.

2. Direct the subgroups to discuss the topic "Communication Problems I Have Encountered" (or you can provide some other relevant topic).

3. Allow approximately 5 to 10 minutes, then stop the discussions.

4. Explain that the subgroups will continue their discussions on the topic, but a new "listening rule" is to be used. The rule states that in order for a person to enter the discussion, he or she must paraphrase or summarize the previous speaker's comments to that person's satisfaction. Once the new speaker has successfully done so, he or she may make any comments. Before the next person enters the discussion, he or she must paraphrase or summarize the previous comments, and so on.

5. Allow approximately 10 minutes for the discussion and then stop the activity.

6. Facilitate a large group discussion by asking the following questions:

    *   Describe your individual feelings during the two discussions.

    *   How well did people listen during the initial discussion? What support do you have for this observation?

    *   Did listening skills improve during the second discussion? What support do you have for this observation?

    *   What are some ways you can improve your own listening skills?

    *   How can you help your customers listen more attentively?

Tongue-Tying Twisters
Word Enunciation

Goal   To communicate clearly and precisely through voice and diction. Participants will practice reading and pronouncing words by saying tongue twisters.

Time Required   Approximately 30 minutes

Group Size   Subgroups of four or five persons each

Materials

- One copy of the Tongue-Tying Twisters Handout for each participant.

- One sheet of paper and a pencil for each participant (optional).

PROCESS

1. Introduce the session by stating that the ability to communicate clearly and concisely is an important part of providing exceptional customer service. This activity is designed to help participants practice these skills in a fun and amusing way.

2. Form subgroups of four or five persons each.

3. Distribute one copy of the handout to each participant.

4. Explain that the members of each group are to read all twelve sentences out loud, first individually in round-robin format and then in unison. Continue until time is called.

5. Allow approximately 10 minutes for the task to be completed, and then call time.

6. *Optional:* Distribute one sheet of paper and a pencil to each participant and ask each person to write an original tongue twister. Direct members of each group to pass their sheets to other members, who will read the twisters out loud.

7. Facilitate a large group discussion by asking the following questions:

   • How difficult was it for you personally to accomplish this task?

   • How did rate of speech affect your ability to speak clearly?

   • How does this relate to your on-the-job performance?

   • Why is clear and concise communication a basic component of exceptional service?

   • What issues may result from poor communication skills?

   • How well did the group perform when the statements were read in unison? Why?

   • How can this aspect of the activity be related to the importance of teamwork in customer service?

   • What steps can be taken to improve the clarity of communication in customer interactions?

TONGUE-TYING TWISTERS HANDOUT

Directions: In round-robin format, each individual will read one statement, and then all statements should be read in unison at least one time. Continue until time is called.

1. Surely Shirley shall sell Sheila's seashells by the seashore.

2. Which witch wishes to switch a witch wristwatch for a Swiss wristwatch?

3. The skunk sat on a stump and thunk the stump stunk, but the stump thunk the skunk stunk.

4. The butter Betty Botter bought could make her batter bitter, so she thought she'd better buy some better butter!

5. Not many an anemone is enamored of an enemy anemone.

6. Five fine Florida florists fried fresh flat flounder fish fillet.

7. A three-toed tree toad loved a two-toed he-toad that lived in a too-tall tree.

8. The instinct of an extinct insect stinks.

9. Growing gray goats graze great green grassy groves.

10. Imagine managing the manger at an imaginary menagerie.

11. Mix a box of mixed biscuits with a boxed biscuit mixer.

12. A cuckoo cookie cook called Cooper could cook cuckoo cookies.

Listen Closely
Responsive Listening

Responsive listening shows a genuine interest in the needs or problems of the customer. Too often people tend to interrupt others because they have made assumptions before gathering all the relevant information. By cultivating good listening skills, service representatives can avoid making mistakes or misreading situations. In addition, listening closely to what the customer says can help prevent problems in the future.

Directions: Evaluate your listening skills and determine where you may need improvement by answering the following questions with YES, NO, or SOMETIMES.

1. Do I judge from the speaker's tone of voice and delivery whether what is being said is worthwhile? _____

2. Do I listen for ideas, underlying feelings, and subtle messages? _____

3. Do I know my biases and put them in perspective? _____

4. Does my mind wander when I listen to someone talk? _____

5. Do I interrupt when someone makes an incorrect statement? _____

6. Do I give good feedback? _____

7. Do I evaluate the logic and credibility of what I hear? _____

8. Do I need to have the last word? _____

9. Do I try to focus the conversation on the other party? _____

10. Do I effectively control the length of the conversation? _____

Review your answers and list your top three STRENGTHS and WEAKNESSES:

Strengths	Weaknesses
1. _____	_____
2. _____	_____
3. _____	_____

How do you feel your strengths help you handle client needs? _____

_____

_____

How do you plan to improve at least one weak area you listed? _____

_____

_____

To the Facilitator

Note that questions on the form alternate between negative and positive attributes. After completion of the assessments, form small groups to discuss some of the strengths and weaknesses identified by individuals and the impact these have on customer service interactions. Conduct a large group discussion based on feedback from the subgroups. Identify ways that listening skills can be improved through both individual efforts and changes to the work environment.

Mind the Message
Communication Processes

Communication is a critical aspect of all human interaction, and it includes both verbal and nonverbal factors. A service representative's ability to communicate effectively has an impact on everything from how information is shared and ideas are perceived to how transactions are conducted and relationships maintained. Being able to satisfy customer expectations and improve perceptions requires solid communication skills in all aspects of the job; that means with customers, the team leader, and colleagues.

Directions: First, think carefully about the general interactions you have within your current work situation in terms of communication (verbal and nonverbal) with customers, peers, and your team leader. Next, complete the following questions about that situation for each of these three areas of interaction.

I think my communication with my customers . . .

Is accurate	1	2	3	4	5	6	7	Is inaccurate
Is easily understood	1	2	3	4	5	6	7	Is not easily understood
Is productive	1	2	3	4	5	6	7	Is unproductive
Is cooperative	1	2	3	4	5	6	7	Is uncooperative
Is relaxed	1	2	3	4	5	6	7	Is strained
Reveals empathy	1	2	3	4	5	6	7	Reveals indifference
Displays competence	1	2	3	4	5	6	7	Displays incompetence
Creates a positive image	1	2	3	4	5	6	7	Creates a negative image
Increases my credibility	1	2	3	4	5	6	7	Decreases my credibility
Gets desired results	1	2	3	4	5	6	7	Does not get desired results

TOTAL: _____

I think my communication with my supervisor (team leader) . . .

Is accurate	1	2	3	4	5	6	7	Is inaccurate
Is easily understood	1	2	3	4	5	6	7	Is not easily understood
Is productive	1	2	3	4	5	6	7	Is unproductive
Is cooperative	1	2	3	4	5	6	7	Is uncooperative
Is relaxed	1	2	3	4	5	6	7	Is strained
Reveals empathy	1	2	3	4	5	6	7	Reveals indifference
Displays competence	1	2	3	4	5	6	7	Displays incompetence
Creates a positive image	1	2	3	4	5	6	7	Creates a negative image
Increases my credibility	1	2	3	4	5	6	7	Decreases my credibility
Gets desired results	1	2	3	4	5	6	7	Does not get desired results

TOTAL: _____

I think my communication with my peers (team members) . . .

Is accurate	1	2	3	4	5	6	7	Is inaccurate
Is easily understood	1	2	3	4	5	6	7	Is not easily understood
Is productive	1	2	3	4	5	6	7	Is unproductive
Is cooperative	1	2	3	4	5	6	7	Is uncooperative
Is relaxed	1	2	3	4	5	6	7	Is strained
Reveals empathy	1	2	3	4	5	6	7	Reveals indifference
Displays competence	1	2	3	4	5	6	7	Displays incompetence
Creates a positive image	1	2	3	4	5	6	7	Creates a negative image
Increases my credibility	1	2	3	4	5	6	7	Decreases my credibility
Gets desired results	1	2	3	4	5	6	7	Does not get desired results

TOTAL: _____

Scoring: Compare each of your three total scores to the following:

          10–24   You have analyzed yourself as a very ineffective communicator.

          25–39   You have analyzed yourself as an ineffective communicator.

          40–54   You see yourself as an effective communicator.

  55 or above   You see yourself as a very effective communicator.

Answer the following questions:

1. In which type of communication are you most effective? Why?

_____

_____

_____

104   101 Ways to Improve Customer Service

2. In which type of communication are you least effective? Why?

_____

_____

_____

3. What actions can you take to become a more effective communicator overall?

_____

_____

_____

_____

_____

_____

To the Facilitator   After completion of the questionnaires, form small groups to discuss the scores and relevant issues that affect communication in the three areas. Ask each subgroup to determine the average scores for the leader and peer sections and enter the data on a flip-chart sheet. Conduct a large group discussion based on these scores and general feedback from the subgroups. Identify specific actions that the team can take to improve the communication process in the work environment.

101 Ways to Improve Customer Service. Copyright © 2007 by John Wiley & Sons, Inc. Reproduced by permission of Pfeiffer, an Imprint of Wiley. www.pfeiffer.com

Probing Points
Questioning

Productive probing skills are based on asking the right questions at the right time. There are two basic types of questions that you can use to gain information from your customers: open ones that get at the big picture and closed ones that focus on details. Effectively moving from one type to the other can keep the communication process under control and provide a means of solving problems more successfully.

Open Questions

- Allow the person to express feelings

- Ask for subjective (personal interpretation) responses

- Cannot be answered with only yes or no

- Allow for longer, more complicated answers

- Open up a subject under discussion to new areas

- Usually start with how, why, what

Closed Questions

- Request specific and factual responses

- Ask for objective (fact-based) responses

- Seek out required information

- Require short answers

- Focus in on specific topics

- Close out new areas for conversation

- Usually start with when, where, who

Directions: Think about some of your own customer interactions. Select **one specific situation** in which you had difficulty obtaining information. Provide one or two examples for each of the following statements and then commit to using the appropriate combination of open and closed questioning in the future.

1. Open question(s) you might use to gain general information at the beginning of the interaction.

2. Open question(s) you would use to encourage the customer to expand on the response to the initial probe.

3. Closed question(s) you would use to uncover more specific information.

4. Closed question(s) you might use to confirm your understanding of something the customer said to you.

> ## To the Facilitator
> After completion of the forms by individuals, form small groups to discuss the examples and their effectiveness in obtaining information and solving problems. Conduct a large group discussion with feedback from each subgroup on their examples and any issues affecting the use of probing skills.

Sound Advice

Voice Quality

Approximately 40 percent of what we communicate verbally to others is perceived through our vocal qualities—that is, tone, pitch, and pace of delivery. An important first step toward improving your voice is to hear yourself as others do.

Directions: Listen to several recordings of your voice on a tape recorder or VCR and then complete the following rating form. Place a check in the appropriate column for each quality listed.

Quality	Major Strength	Strength	Weakness	Major Weakness
Projects confidence				
Projects enthusiasm				
Projects optimism				
Projects sincerity				
Projects calmness				
Voice is not too high or too low				
Voice is not too loud or too soft				
Speaking rate is not too fast or too slow				

Review any weak areas and identify some actions that you can take to improve these qualities.

_____

_____

_____

_____

_____

_____

To the Facilitator   Make tape recorder and/or VCR equipment and tapes available to group members, either in the classroom setting or in an office space that is accessible to all; or ask individuals to perform the recordings at home. If the recordings are to be done as part of a class, they can be especially effective when performed as a part of a role-play exercise. A group discussion can be formed around specific actions that can be taken to improve weak areas.

Crossing the Border
International Communication

Individual

When you communicate with people outside of the United States, they can find it very confusing and frustrating to encounter words or phases that are unfamiliar to them. Your choice of words can even be offensive in many cases. Also, don't forget to drop the company jargon and acronyms that have little or no meaning to anyone outside your organization.

ACTIONS

- Here are some examples of general phrases of which you should steer clear:

  - *Slang:* two-bit, nuts and bolts, ballpark figure, kick off, take it easy, the pits

  - *Buzzwords:* Mickey Mouse, no strings attached, monkey around, across the board, game plan, ramp up, touch base

  - *Clichés:* pay through the nose, beat a dead horse, dog-eat-dog, rule of thumb, full steam ahead, bury the hatchet, easy as pie, all over the map

● Make a list of jargon, slang, buzzwords, and acronyms that are specific to your organization. Post it in a prominent place and check your communication (written and verbal) to make sure you are not using them.

E-Service
Electronic Communication

Individual

The Internet has created a wonderful way to keep your customers instantaneously up-to-date. However, how this powerful tool is used to stay in touch with the customer can make the difference between success and failure. When you use e-mail as a communication device, be sure to follow these guidelines to make sure that your customer stays informed in an efficient and professional manner.

ACTIONS

- The subject line of an e-mail is one of the most important parts of your message. It tells the recipient in an instant what to expect in the body of the e-mail. To keep your communications with customers on track, always check the subject line before you send an e-mail. If the subject has changed, change the subject line.

- When sending attachment files larger than 500K, let your customer know that the file is large and may take some time to download. This won't make the downloading time pass more quickly, but at least the customer will know the cause of the delay. Your customer will appreciate the warning.

- Whenever you write an e-mail, ask yourself, "Who else needs to know about this?" Then determine whether a Cc (carbon copy) or Bcc (blind carbon copy) is more appropriate. You want to Cc your supervisor or manager to keep him or her informed about a particular correspondence, but you may want to use Bcc if your boss doesn't want an e-mail address put in print.

technique **31**

Attention, Please

Keeping the Customer's Attention

Some service-related problems relate directly to a misunderstanding of the information provided by the service representative to the customer. One of the reasons this occurs is because the customer has not paid close attention to the details of the conversation. This is especially true when the interaction occurs over the telephone; the customer loses the face-to-face engagement of body language and must rely totally on voice and message content. Some of the more common pitfalls and suggestions to remedy these situations are described in the following table.

Pitfall	Remedy
People are impatient when they listen.	Make your main point at the beginning of your conversation. Keep your information short and specific.
People jump to conclusions before you are finished talking.	Stress a benefit at the beginning of what you say and make it too attractive to reject. Hearing what they will gain gives customers some perspective on the conversation, lets them know what point you are trying to make, and tells them why they should listen.
People typically fully concentrate for only approximately 15 seconds at a time. Their minds may wander for a few seconds and then they pay attention to the speaker again.	Present only one idea at a time. Adapt your important points to meet the individual customer's focus of attention.
It takes work to remember something. Even if people listen closely, they don't automatically store what you have said in their minds.	Promote an ongoing, two-way dialogue and check for understanding. Periodically get reactions to what you have said. See if their understanding of the information matches what you are trying to get across.
Even if people remember what you have said, they won't necessarily do anything about it.	Ask questions that will get them to visualize doing something with the information. These questions might involve ways they will use the information or what they will do next.

Return Policy
Feedback Guidelines

There are many benefits to giving and receiving constructive feedback. It reduces uncertainty, helps solve problems, builds trust, strengthens relationships, and, most important, improves work quality. From day-to-day interactions with customers and colleagues to formal performance reviews, feedback that is specific, nonjudgmental, and timely creates more effective communication processes in support of continuous improvement efforts.

Giving Feedback

1. Focus on the behavior of the individual or the group, not on the personality or character.

2. Make it specific (what, when, where, and so on).

3. *Describe* the person's behavior; do not *judge* it.

4. Direct the feedback at behavior that can be changed, not at permanent characteristics of an individual.

5. Make it timely, either at the moment the behavior is occurring or as soon afterward as possible.

6. Remember that people are uncomfortable receiving feedback, even if you are handling it the best way possible.

7. Whether the person agrees to continue (positive feedback) or to change (negative feedback), express your appreciation for his or her listening to your concern.

Receiving Feedback

1. Actively listen to the person's description of your behavior and his or her recommendations to continue what you are doing or suggested changes that would be helpful. (This might be difficult!)

2. Do not get defensive; trust that the intent of the feedback is to help you, not hurt you.

3. Paraphrase or summarize the feedback to make sure you have heard it correctly.

4. Give the feedback serious consideration. Do not dismiss it as irrelevant or unimportant.

5. Communicate to the person any changes in his or her behavior that may be needed to help you change.

6. Whether or not you use the feedback, express appreciation to the other person for caring enough about the relationship to give you the feedback, and request that he or she continue to do so.

Six Degrees of Persuasion
Influencing Through Listening

In active listening, the listener remains silent so as to organize what the speaker is saying (main ideas and key words) and then to analyze and compare what is being said to what the listener thinks or knows. Remaining silent also allows the listener to hear the feelings and emotions behind the words so that it is possible to try to understand the speaker's point of view. Active listening means that the listener should refrain from interrupting, arguing, passing judgment, or jumping to conclusions.

The following guidelines incorporate the use of active listening skills as a means of persuading others to accept your point of view.

1. Understand the other person's point of view.   You cannot expect to persuade someone of anything until you clearly understand that person's present position and attitude. Nobody likes to be out-talked. You can persuade people only if they are willing to listen to you. The best way to get them to listen to you is first to listen to them.

2. Don't jump to conclusions.   Never assume that you know what someone else needs or what he or she is thinking or is going to say next. By jumping to conclusions, you cut off listening, even if for a few seconds, because it takes only a few moments to miss some important information. Listening is done with an open mind. When your mind is closed, you merely hear.

3. Be respectful.   Without an attitude of respect, you might hear what others are saying, but you are not likely to really listen to them. It will be evident if you don't respect the person you are trying to persuade, and this can contribute to increased resistance to your opinion. Respect for other opinions and ideas can help you understand and present your own interests better.

4. Control your emotions.   Once your emotions get out of control, you are more likely to jump to conclusions and become judgmental. You will find yourself not listening carefully, and this in turn may fuel the fire for the other person to argue with you. Once this happens, it may become difficult for the other party to listen to you rationally.

5. Repeat to clarify.   Repeat what you think the other person said to be sure that you understood the message correctly. The speaker will be receptive once he or she sees that you are making an effort to comprehend exactly what is being said rather than arguing or disagreeing. You will find that you are able to listen more carefully when you acknowledge beforehand that you will try to articulate your perception of the other's point of view.

6. Keep the dialogue going.   It is important to keep the dialogue going so that the other person is discouraged from fighting or shutting down. Because people seldom argue on a completely rational basis, it's necessary to acknowledge the emotions and opinions that affect a discussion.

Planning

Because companies naturally have limited resources available in terms of employees, data acquisition, supplies, equipment, and so forth, planning is a critical factor in providing exceptional customer service. Successful service and quality improvement efforts require solid preparation and management. Planning creates the structure necessary for the customer service function to operate, particularly as it relates to task completion. It affects the organization's ability to provide quality customer service in terms of employee knowledge, goal setting, standards, processes and procedures, functionality of service and products, change management, organization, documentation, and continuous improvement.

For most customers, reliability is considered to be the core of quality service. Therefore, an organization's goal is to deliver products or services to customers in an efficient and timely manner without error. This requires service representatives who are resourceful, responsive, and, most important, accurate. They must listen carefully to requests, follow instructions, research information promptly, keep to agreed-on schedules, and solve any problems that arise.

Customers base important decisions on the information they receive from organizational representatives. Service providers therefore need to be well informed about the company's products and services as well as be aware of the various processes that promote quality service. Training must occur right from the beginning and be maintained continuously so that service employees acquire the skills and abilities to communicate the spirit of customer service that the organization wants.

Knowledgeable service representatives can offer clients a true understanding of the company's ability and desire to satisfy their needs. One of the quickest ways to lose a customer is to give the false impression that the service provider knows the answer when he or she doesn't. This means that service providers must rely on a variety of resources—from job aids and databases to the knowledge and experience of coworkers—to access information.

As a competitive economy causes organizations to do more with less, scarce resources force everyone to combine forces to achieve success. Further, because service representatives often must juggle many different jobs at once, they may need to get help with the overall workload. Therefore, it is especially important for them to recognize when to rely on the expertise of others or when it is necessary to pass on work for others to do. Delegating tasks helps create an empowered environment while confronting time demands.

Oftentimes, the general pressure of deadlines can decrease the amount of work that employees might accomplish as well as diminish the quality of the service that they provide to customers. However, proper work planning, organization, documentation, and time management can eliminate the negative forces of urgency. If mistakes do occur, it is especially critical to keep a record of the errors made, the causes, and their solutions. Reviewing this list personally and then sharing the information with supervisors or managers can help prevent recurrence of the problems.

Service representatives need to take every occasion possible to learn more about the intricacies of their company's business. Examining current workplace operating processes and procedures on an ongoing basis gives individuals and teams a way to provide the organization with information to plan an effective continuous improvement approach.

Color Quest

Limited Resources

Goal
To identify how limited resources affect performance, goal setting, strategic planning, and negotiations. Participants will select a candy color and collect the most pieces possible.

Time Required
Approximately 30 to 45 minutes

Group Size
Six to eight subgroups with no more than six persons each

Materials

- One fun-size packet of M&M's® candies for each participant

- A flip chart and felt-tipped markers for recording

- Prizes for the winning group (optional)

● ●

PROCESS

1. Form six to eight subgroups with no more than six persons each. Distribute one packet of M&M's to each participant.

2. Explain that each subgroup must collect one color of candy, obtaining as many pieces as possible. The group with the largest number of the same color will be declared the winner. Signal for the task to begin.

3. Depending on the total number of subgroups and the amount of interaction taking place, allow sufficient time (approximately 10 minutes) for participants to mingle and trade, then signal for the activity to stop.

4. Ask each subgroup to count the total number of candies in the color selected. On the flip chart, record the candy color and the total number of pieces collected for each subgroup. Announce the winning group and give out prizes if you choose to do so.

5. Facilitate a large group discussion by asking the following questions:

   • What factors were considered in selecting your group's candy color? Did the original selection change as the task progressed? Why or why not?

   • How did limited resources affect your group's performance? Did the availability of resources change your group's goals as the activity progressed? Why or why not?

   • What are some examples of how workplace goals change as a reflection of the availability of resources? How does this affect a group's strategic planning process?

   • How did you personally react to changes in conditions? How did others in your group react? As conditions changed, what did your group do to adjust?

   • What role does interdependence across groups play in accomplishing tasks?

   • In preparing for strategic planning or negotiations, how important are your assumptions (or research of competition and market conditions)? What happens when your assumptions are wrong? How do you adjust?

   • How does this activity relate to specific conditions in your workplace?

Commercial Appeal
Product or Service Offerings

Goal   To examine functionality of product or service offerings in meeting customer needs. Participants will create a commercial for a product or service that nobody would want.

Time Required   Approximately 1 hour

Group Size   Subgroups of four or five persons each, with a maximum of thirty participants

Materials

- One index card and a pencil for each participant

- One poster board sheet and several felt-tipped markers for each subgroup

- A box of assorted items (for example, office supplies, clothing, toys, books, pictures, and so forth)

● ●

PROCESS

1. Distribute one index card and a pencil to each participant.

2. Ask the participants to think of a product or service that they think nobody would want and to describe it on the card provided. Give the following examples or something similar: "a shampoo that smells like a skunk" or "a vacuum cleaner that sprays out dirt."

3. Allow several minutes for task completion and then collect the completed cards.

4. Form subgroups of four or five persons each.

5. Shuffle the product index cards and randomly distribute one to each subgroup. Provide one poster board sheet and several felt-tipped markers to each subgroup.

6. Explain that each group is to create a brief television commercial of approximately 1 minute featuring the product or service listed on the assigned card. Indicating the box of assorted items, tell the groups that they can use anything from the box as well as the poster board to enhance the message of the commercial, but that this is an option and not a requirement for the task.

7. Allow approximately 20 minutes for the subgroups to work on the task, giving a 5-minute and then a 1-minute warning before time expires.

8. Ask each subgroup in turn to present its commercial.

9. Facilitate a large group discussion by asking the following questions:

   • What characteristics of the product did your group emphasize? Why?

   • What about a commercial makes its message believable? Why?

   • What role does creativity play in advertising?

   • How does this affect how the message is received by the audience?

   • How do you determine the needs of your customers?

   • Is your company providing products or services that are no longer needed by your customers? If so, what are they?

   • Can these products or services be changed so that they meet customer needs? If so, how?

   • How might your company better advertise its products and services?

Flow Motion

Work Process Improvement

Goal   To look for ways to improve a current work process. Participants will create a flow chart to document a work process and make suggestions for improvement.

Time Required   Approximately 1½ to 2 hours

Group Size   Subgroups of three or four persons each from an intact service team, with a maximum of twenty participants

Materials

- One sheet of newsprint paper and two felt-tipped markers in different colors for each group

- One copy of the Flow Motion Worksheet and a pencil for each participant

- Masking tape for posting newsprint sheets

PROCESS

1. Introduce the session by stating that quality depends on analyzing current work processes to ensure that they are most effective in reaching the desired outcome. The first part of this analysis is breaking down the process into the steps required to get the job done. Explain that work processes should be reviewed periodically to ensure that modifications are being made as necessary.

2. Form subgroups of three or four persons each.

3. Distribute one copy of the worksheet and a pencil to each participant.

4. Ask each subgroup to select a current work process that is complex enough to involve several steps. Explain that each group will have 20 minutes to analyze this process by completing the worksheet with as much detail as possible.

5. Give a 5-minute warning before time expires, and then stop group work after 20 minutes. Distribute one sheet of newsprint paper and two felt-tipped markers in different colors to each group.

6. Instruct the groups to create a flow chart by writing each step of the work process in order on the newsprint sheet using one color marker.

7. Allow approximately 10 to 15 minutes, giving a 2-minute warning before time expires, and then stop the groups.

8. Tell the groups that they have 20 minutes to identify those steps they feel should be improved and why, using the second color marker to indicate revisions on the original flow chart. As a guide, groups should focus on the last two areas of the worksheet (Necessary Resources and Driving Forces).

9. Allow approximately 20 minutes, giving a 2-minute warning before time expires, and then stop the groups.

10. Provide masking tape and have the groups post their sheets. Ask each group in turn to present its flow chart and identify the steps that group members thought needed improvement and the reasons why. Encourage other participants to ask questions for clarification.

11. Facilitate a large group discussion by asking:

    • What specific actions can the service team take to support process improvement?

FLOW MOTION WORKSHEET

Process Name:

Purpose:

Process Steps:

Results and Consequences:

Necessary Resources:

Driving Forces:

Hardware
Classifying Resources

 Goal To develop ways to classify available resources for accessibility. Participants will place hardware items into categories for ease of identification.

Time Required   Approximately 1 hour

Group Size   Three to six subgroups with three to five persons each

 ## Materials

- One identical set of fifty varied hardware items (washers, nails, screws, bolts, nuts, and other small objects) for each subgroup

- One plastic bag and tie closure for each subgroup

- Twelve index cards and a felt-tipped pen for each subgroup

- A list of search items for the facilitator

- Flip chart and felt-tipped marker for recording scores

PROCESS

1. Prior to the session, place an assortment of fifty hardware items into a plastic bag and tie it closed; each subgroup should have an identical set of items. Prepare a list that describes eight to ten *specific* items from the collection that will be used for a group search (for example, "a 2-inch, flat-head nail"). Prepare a flip chart with a number for each group participating in the activity.

2. Form subgroups of three to five persons each and provide a number designation to each group.

3. Distribute one bag of hardware items, twelve index cards, and a felt-tipped pen to each subgroup.

4. Explain that each subgroup is to develop a system of organizing these items so that a customer would be able to find what he or she needed easily. Using the index cards, each subgroup is to create a label for each category of hardware to facilitate the customer's search. *Note:* Groups may decide to label their objects in general or more specifically. For example, some may use "nails" as the category, whereas others may make subcategories as to nail size (1-inch, 2-inch, and so on) and/or type (flat-head, rounded, and so on).

5. Allow approximately 15 minutes to complete the task, giving a 2-minute warning before time expires.

6. Explain that each subgroup will send a member to another group to locate a specific item that will be announced. The customer will raise his or her hand when the correct item is found, and the group that was able to complete the transaction by locating the correct object will be awarded 5 points. This process will be repeated several times, and scoring will be kept on the flip chart by the facilitator.

7. Start the first round by asking each subgroup to select a member to act as the customer. Announce the first item on the prepared list and signal for these customers to proceed to any available group and ask for an item. Record five points for the winning group under the appropriate designation on the flip chart. Repeat this process several times by announcing a new item for each successive round.

8. Facilitate a large group discussion by asking the following questions:

- How well did your group's system of categorizing the materials work for finding specific items? Did your group alter its system as the rounds of play continued? Why or why not? If you changed anything, did the new system work better or worse? Why?

- How can we relate this activity to the workplace in terms of making products and services accessible to the customer?

- How well do your current workplace processes and procedures meet the needs of your customers? Why?

- How does the presence of competitors influence the way in which we "do business"?

- What are some specific actions that can be implemented to improve your company's customer experience in terms of user-friendliness?

Heads and Tails
Optimizing Resources

Goal   To optimize the use of available resources. Participants will form six-letter words by combining appropriate three-letter word pairs.

Time Required   Approximately 30 to 45 minutes

Group Size   Ten to twenty participants

Materials

- Twenty large adhesive shipping labels and a felt-tipped marker

- One copy of the Heads and Tails Answer Sheet for the facilitator

- One sheet of blank paper and a pencil for each participant

● ●

PROCESS

1. Prior to the session, prepare the labels by using large block letters to print the following word pairs on separate labels.

SEA – EGO	CUT – PEN	OFF – LET	IMP – LED
RAT – PET	ARC – ORE	TAR – HER	GAL – ACE
RED – ION	CAR – DON	BUT – ONE	MAN – GET
SON – HEM	PAL – TON	DAM – ART	PAR – ICE
MAR – SON	FOR – NET	PEA – RED	ANT—AGE

2. At the beginning of the session, place one or two labels (depending on the number of participants) on the back of each person.

3. Distribute one sheet of paper and a pencil to each participant.

4. Explain that each label bears two three-letter words. The word on the left is a "head" and the one on the right is a "tail." When each head is joined to a particular tail, it will form a six-letter word. There are two rules: (1) participants are not allowed to merely make a list of the heads and tails and then match the words, but must find the complete word match before listing it, and (2) no head or tail may be used more than once no matter how well it may match up again.

5. Tell the participants that they are to walk around the room without talking, looking at the labels on the backs of others while trying to match up the appropriate heads with the tails. The resulting twenty words are to be written on the paper provided.

6. Allow approximately 7 to 10 minutes and then stop the activity.

7. Determine who had formed the most words and ask the person(s) to read the list(s). Verify the answers against the list of words on the answer sheet.

8. Facilitate a large group discussion by asking the following questions:

    • What process did you use to determine the appropriate word combinations?

    • Was it necessary to make any changes in the process as you progressed through the task?

- Why were some words more difficult to form than others? *(Recognizable three-letter words affect the ability to blend into other words, such as arc + her to form "archer")*

- How did you determine the words that were on your own back so that you could complete the task?

- Why is planning such an important part of utilizing available resources?

- What actions can you take to plan for the optimal use of workplace resources?

HEADS AND TAILS ANSWER SHEET

1. anthem   ANT – HEM

2. archer   ARC – HER

3. button   BUT – TON

4. carpet   CAR – PET

5. cutlet   CUT – LET

6. dampen   DAM – PEN

7. forego   FOR – EGO

8. galore   GAL – ORE

9. impart   IMP – ART

10. manage   MAN – AGE

11. marred   MAR – RED

12. office   OFF – ICE

13. palace   PAL – ACE

14. pardon   PAR – DON

15. pealed   PEA – LED

16. ration   RAT – ION

17. redone   RED – ONE

18. season   SEA – SON

19. sonnet   SON – NET

20. target   TAR – GET

Last Straw

Goal Setting and Resources

Goal To examine the impact of goal setting and resource utilization on task completion. Participants will work in groups to build the highest freestanding structure from drinking straws using the least costly resources.

Time Required Approximately 45 minutes to 1 hour

Group Size Subgroups of three to five persons each, with a maximum of twenty-five participants

Materials

- Several boxes of bendable drinking straws, paper clips, rubber bands, pins, and masking tape

- One copy of the Last Straw Requisition Form and a pencil for each subgroup

- A measuring tape or yardstick

- Scissors

● ●

PROCESS

1. Prior to the session, place the materials (straws, paper clips, rubber bands, pins, tape) on a table that is easily accessible to all groups.

2. Form subgroups of three to five persons each.

3. Explain that teams will attempt to construct a freestanding framework of drinking straws that is taller than any other team's structure using the least costly set of materials. The winner will be determined using the calculation formula of $5 per inch of height minus the total cost of materials. Additional building materials include paper clips, rubber bands, pins, and masking tape. Teams will have 10 minutes to plan and 20 minutes to carry out the construction phase.

> Note   You may wish to allow teams to discover how to join the straws, or you can demonstrate some ways in which the straws can be joined: squeeze one end of a straw and place it inside another straw; use pins or masking tape to hold straws together; use rubber bands to bind straws where they intersect; or connect them with paper clips, as shown in the figure.

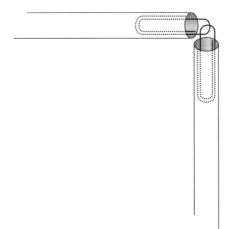

4. Distribute one copy of the requisition form and a pencil to each subgroup.

5. Allow teams 10 minutes to plan and complete the requisition form. Collect the forms and distribute the materials to each team as requested.

6. Signal for the construction to begin. Time the activity for 20 minutes, giving a 3-minute warning before time expires. During this time, use the flip chart to record the cost of materials purchased by each team; keep the information concealed.

7. Measure each structure and record the height for each team on the flip chart next to the cost. Determine the winner by using the calculation formula of $5 per inch for height minus the total cost of materials.

8. Facilitate a large group discussion by asking the following questions:

   - How did your team develop a plan for the structure?

   - Did your team need to alter its original plan during the actual construction? Why or why not?

   - What was your team's goal for the structure's height? Was the goal met? Why or why not?

   - How did the cost of materials figure into your plan? Was the estimate realistic? Why?

   - If you were able to do the task again, what, if anything, would you have done differently?

   - What role did creativity play in accomplishing the task?

   - How does this activity relate to the actual completion of tasks in the workplace?

   - What can your service team do differently to improve its work performance in terms of goal setting? In terms of resource utilization?

Source: Adapted from Ukens, L. L. (1995). Skyscrapers. In *Working together* (pp. 132–134). San Francisco: Pfeiffer.

LAST STRAW REQUISITION FORM

Directions: Indicate the number of each supply item that will be purchased and calculate the final cost for the materials. Submit this form to the facilitator prior to the construction phase.

Quantity	Item	Unit	Price	Cost
	Straws	Each	$10.00	
	Rubber bands	Each	$2.00	
	Pins	Each	$1.00	
	Paper clips	Each	$2.00	
	Masking tape	Inch	$3.00	
			Total Cost	

On Target
Goal Alignment

Goal To align individual, team, and organizational goals. Participants will identify and compare individual and organizational expectations of the service team.

Time Required Approximately 45 minutes to 1 hour

Group Size Subgroups of three to five persons each. This activity is best used within an intact service team.

Materials

- One copy of the On Target Worksheet and a pencil for each participant

- Two newsprint sheets and a felt-tipped marker for the facilitator

- Masking tape for posting newsprint sheets

● ●

PROCESS

1. Prior to the session, prepare the two newsprint sheets by placing a heading of Individual on one and Organization on the other. Use masking tape to post the sheets.

2. Introduce the session by stating that common goals help teams function better and that support for those goals comes from aligning individual, team, and organizational expectations.

3. Distribute one copy of the worksheet and a pencil to each participant.

4. Ask the participants to think about the two questions and instruct them to record their responses on the worksheet. Allow approximately 5 to 10 minutes to complete the task.

5. Form subgroups of three to five persons each.

6. Invite group members to share their responses with one another and allow approximately 10 minutes for discussion.

7. Using the two prepared newsprint sheets, record several examples each for individual and organization expectations.

8. Facilitate a general discussion by asking the following questions:

   • Did members of your subgroup identify similar individual expectations? If so, what kind? If not, what differences were evident?

   • Did members of your subgroup identify similar organization expectations? If so, what kind? If not, what differences were evident?

   • In general, how close was the fit between the individual expectations and the organizational expectations?

   • Were there any general discrepancies between the two sets of expectations? If so, what kind?

   • What are some reasons that discrepancies like these occur?

   • How do such discrepancies affect the functioning of a service team? Give some examples.

   • How can a service team work together to identify team goals that align both individual and organizational expectations?

ON TARGET WORKSHEET

1. In general, what do YOU expect your service team, as a group, to be able to accomplish?

2. In general, what do you think the ORGANIZATION expects your service team to accomplish?

View from the Top
Personal Change Management

Goal To explore how change influences personal actions. Participants will print the word "change" while focusing on the reflected view in a mirror.

Time Required Approximately 15 minutes

Group Size Any number of individuals

Materials

- One pocket mirror, one index card, and a pencil for each participant

- A newsprint sheet and felt-tipped marker for facilitator

- Masking tape for posting newsprint sheet

PROCESS

1. Prior to the session, use a felt-tipped marker to print the word "change" on the newsprint sheet and post the sheet prominently on a wall using masking tape.

2. Distribute one mirror, one index card, and a pencil to each participant.

3. Explain that each person is to first place the index card on a flat surface and then position the mirror so that the card is reflected in the mirror. Referring to the posted newsprint sheet, tell the participants that they are to print the word "change" in small letters while *keeping their eyes on the mirror only*.

4. Allow several minutes for completion of the task, observing the progress made by the participants, and then call time.

5. Facilitate a large group discussion by asking the following questions:

    *   How did you feel while you were attempting to complete the task?

    *   Did you rely on others to help guide you in the process? Why or why not?

    *   Why do you think it was difficult for you to print a word that was familiar to you?

    *   How can you relate this activity to the concept of change?

    *   What role does perception play in managing change?

    *   Why is it so important for service providers to see issues from the customer's point of view?

    *   What actions can you take to help the customer change his or her position on an issue?

    *   What actions can you take to help yourself manage change more effectively?

Desk Stress
Organization

If a work space is cluttered and disorganized, it is highly probable that information, files, and other important papers are getting lost in the chaos. This means that you may not be at your most efficient when your customers need your assistance. Also, many customers assume that a messy desk or office means that the entire organization is haphazard, if not completely dysfunctional. When a disorderly desk impairs your ability to function or influences customer perception negatively, it's time to commit to a better business practice.

Directions: Think about the current condition of your work desk and answer each question truthfully by circling YES or NO. Next, take some time to analyze your weaknesses and make plans for improvement.

1. Do you have an overflowing in-basket on your desk?   YES   NO

2. Do you keep activities recorded on more than one calendar?   YES   NO

3. Are there more than three file projects on your desk?   YES   NO

4. Are you frequently unable to locate things on your desk?   YES   NO

5. Do you keep piles of unfinished reading on your desk?   YES   NO

6. Do you write phone messages and reminders on scraps of paper?   YES   NO

7. Do you leave work each day with piles of paper on your desk?   YES   NO

8. Are others afraid to leave important documents on your desk?   YES   NO

9. Are others unable to find items on your desk if you aren't there?   YES   NO

10. Are you known for having a messy desk?   YES   NO

Total of YES responses: _____

Scoring:

> 7–10   Your messy desk is hindering productivity and could affect how others regard your work.
>
> 4–6   You might be a candidate for desk stress.
>
> 1–3   You are winning the war over desk stress.

Help Is at Hand.   Use the four D's to overcome desk stress:

- DO it.

  - Handle each piece of paper only once. If action is needed at a later date, file it.

- DATE it.

  - Record the date the item was received and when you will act on it.

- DELEGATE it.

  - Prioritize the work and hand it off to the most appropriate person.

- DISCARD it.

  - If it's not important, throw it away.

Your Goals

1. _____

   _____

2. _____

   _____

3. _____

   _____

To the Facilitator   After the questionnaires have been completed, form small groups to discuss the ratings and identify instances where a disorganized work space had a negative impact on customer service. Conduct a large group discussion based on feedback from the subgroups. Brainstorm a list of specific actions that can be taken to overcome desk stress on the job.

Pass It On
Delegation

Good customer service sometimes means we need to rely on the expertise of others or to get help with the workload. Some examples of when to delegate include when a client is transitioned into a customer service support role or when someone else needs to follow up on a customer complaint. No matter why we have to do it, delegating requires us to use a flexible yet structured approach.

Directions: Take the following survey to find out how good of a delegator you are currently, while taking note of the ways in which you can improve for the future.

	YES	NO
1. Do you believe that others can do a job as well as you can?	_____	_____
Know that different *doesn't necessarily mean better or worse.*		
2. Do you trust your coworkers to handle job assignments?	_____	_____
Trust the ability of others to do the work.		
3. Do you avoid being a perfectionist?	_____	_____
Establish a standard and a time frame for reaching it.		

	YES	NO

4. Do you give job instructions effectively?   ____ ____

Give enough information to complete the job successfully.

5. Do you enjoy managing work rather than just doing it?   ____ ____

Know your true interests in doing versus managing.

6. Do you believe that making mistakes is part of learning?   ____ ____

Encourage staff to accept assignments by viewing their mistakes as learning experiences.

7. Do you follow up with people after delegating?   ____ ____

Build in checkpoints to identify potential problems.

8. Do you avoid crisis management?   ____ ____

Allow time for planning or prioritizing.

9. When delegating, do you leave the person alone to do the work?   ____ ____

Ask questions, expect answers, and assist but don't take over.

10. Do you provide support through feedback and actions?   ____ ____

Provide resources and communicate expectations.

Areas for Improvement

_____   _____

_____   _____

To the Facilitator   After the questionnaires have been completed, form small groups to discuss some of the improvement areas that were identified by individuals. Conduct a large group discussion regarding specific actions that can be taken in the work environment to facilitate employees' ability to delegate.

Flag It
File Management

Individual

If you have customers who have encountered a problem with your company, they will be willing to forgive you if their problem was resolved quickly and appropriately. However, if they face the same mistake or something else goes wrong, they may not be willing to forgive you the second time. By taking some time to document problem situations, you can stay better aware of your customers' unique experiences. This extra attention will help keep customers from defecting to your competitors.

ACTIONS

- Flag the files of those customers who have made complaints or experienced problems.

- Write detailed notes so that any service provider who accesses the file can understand the situation.

- Whenever possible, review the file *before* you speak with the customer.

Just the Fax
Fax Information File

Leader

More times than necessary, employees can waste precious time accessing customer files in order to locate a correct fax number. Here's a suggestion to help make your office more efficient by eliminating this potentially frustrating time waster.

● ●

ACTION

Create a customer fax directory:

1. Obtain a small alphabetized Rolodex unit.

2. Provide employees with several blank Rolodex cards and ask them to complete a card with the name and fax numbers for each of their regular customer contacts, both internal and external.

3. Collect the cards, check for duplicates (make sure numbers are the same), and then file them in the appropriate letter sections of the Rolodex.

4. Place the Rolodex unit next to the fax machine to be used as a reference directory whenever someone doesn't have a number.

5. Make it a rule that new numbers are to be entered as necessary.

Library Dues
Development Resources

Leader

One way to keep your service representatives performing to their highest ability is to create a lending library that supports self-directed learning. It shows that the organization values the development of its employees and helps create an empowered working environment that increases job commitment.

● ●

ACTION

Create a learning resource lending library:

1. Set aside a separate small room or, if this is unavailable, a bookcase that is conveniently located in Human Resources or within a department.

2. Collect a variety of books, audiotapes, videotapes, and magazine articles that aid employees in performing their jobs more effectively.

3. Include the following topics: change management, communication, conflict resolution, customer service, goal setting, managing diversity, presentations, meeting facilitation, negotiation, problem solving, quality issues, stress, and time management.

4. Use a sign-out sheet or computer database file that includes such information as the person's name, department, e-mail address, and date.

5. Put a time limit on how long the material can be kept out (2 weeks is a good standard) and send a reminder e-mail message if materials become overdue.

6. Keep the information current by adding new resources.

Memory Ticklers
Information Recall

Individual

The ability to remember certain facts and procedures can be an important part of providing efficient and effective customer service. Remembering customer names and the details of transactions helps underscore the uniqueness of each customer interaction. Although you don't necessarily need to memorize certain processes and procedures, the quicker you are able to perform them, the faster you will be able to help your customers. Here are some techniques you can use to help improve your memory skills.

ACTIONS

- You can train yourself to remember names, lists, and information by "linking" pictures in your mind. If you want to remember a sequence of steps to perform a task or complete a process, try to form a strong image in your mind of each item in the sequence. For example, the basic steps in resolving conflict and their possible identifying images are as follows: identify issues (MAGNIFYING GLASS), ask questions for clarification (QUESTION MARK), brainstorm possible solutions (LIGHT BULB), agree on solution (TARGET), implement solution (ARROW), and follow up (CHECK MARK). When all the image steps are linked together, you will be able to remember the entire process. If you have forgotten steps, rethink that specific part of the link.

- Mnemonics are verbal devices that help you remember things. (They are named after the Greek goddess of memory, Mnemosyne.) There are lots of rhyming mnemonics—for example, "*i* before *e* except after *c*, or when it sounds like *a*, as in neighbor and weigh." There are also mnemonics that use the first letter of each word as a reminder. "Roy G. Biv" helps you remember the colors of the rainbow in order: red, orange, yellow, green, blue, indigo, and violet. Initial-letter mnemonics are useful for remembering lists or facts. Make up silly words using the first letters of the words you want to remember.

- Use "cheat sheets" with key words and/or phrases in sequential order for performing a process or procedure that requires several steps.

- Keep a pad of paper handy to take notes when you are talking to others, either in person or on the telephone.

New Kids on the Block
Orientation

Leader

New employees need time to adjust to the environment and any required processes or procedures. It is especially important to keep this in mind when you bring new representatives on board. You want to be sure that your customers receive the consistently outstanding service they expect, so don't put your new service providers in situations that they can't handle.

• •

ACTIONS

- Introduce your new service providers to one new skill set at a time by prioritizing all the skills you want them to master and teaching them in that order.

- Pair up new employees with experienced representatives for the first few weeks on the job.

- Provide new employees with all the data and resources they will need to perform their jobs.

- If possible, route customers according to the new representative's acquired product knowledge and skill sets.

- Reframe mistakes made by new employees into learning opportunities by analyzing and discussing what can be done to correct things next time.

To Do or Not to Do
To-Do Lists

Individual

Staying organized can help tremendously in a job that relies on time management and information accessibility. People often rely on to-do lists to keep themselves organized and efficient. However, for a to-do list to be effective, you may need to follow some simple guidelines.

ACTIONS

- Make using a to-do list a habit. Don't skip even one day, or you'll end up disturbing the routine.

- Put only important items on the list. Putting routine tasks on the list is counterproductive when it gives the impression that you have too much to accomplish.

- Place the items in priority order (A = must do, B = should do, C = nice to do) and then rank each item within the category in order of importance.

- Check off items on the list during the day. This helps you feel that you are accomplishing things and can help reduce stress.

- Rewrite the list when it becomes messy or illegible from notes or checking off items. It will become shorter, and you'll feel that you are getting things done!

- Keep the list somewhere you can see it or access it easily.

- Use online software, such as Outlook, that can help you follow up with flags and color coding.

- Coordinate your to-do list with a datebook, keeping all information on only one calendar.

techinque 50

Setting the Bar
Service Standards

Customer service standards are created for employees to follow to ensure that the quality of service to all customers meets or exceeds their expectations. Standards are based on observable behaviors, which provide the basis for evaluating individual performance. To begin the process of setting standards for your own team, follow these guidelines.

- Define the subdivisions of your service sequences as though they were chapters in a book.

- Map out the basic steps in chronological order for each sequence.

- Determine key value-added service qualities that enhance the customer's experience for each step.

- Convert the steps and enhancers into meaningful service standards.

- Clarify that the standards are consistent with the organization's mission statement.

Next, use the following eight criteria to make your service standards more effective. Don't forget to periodically review your standards to determine if they need revision.

1. Specific
2. Concise

3. Measurable

4. Based on customer requirements

5. Defined as personal, product, and procedural

6. Included in job descriptions and performance reviews

7. Jointly created with staff members

8. Fairly and equitably enforced

Following are examples of general service qualities that were turned into specific service standards.

Service Quality	Service Standard
Answer the phone promptly.	Answer the phone within three rings.
Return calls in a timely manner.	Return all calls within 24 hours.
Show empathy with an upset customer.	Express awareness of the customer's concerns through positive words and tone of voice.
Be personally responsible for helping a customer.	Provide the customer with your name, department, and phone number.
Dress appropriately for work.	Wear your full uniform at all times, including the tie and cap.
Be knowledgeable about the company.	Utilize the database of company products and services when providing information to the customer.

Note   This information is intended to guide the group leader or manager in developing appropriate service standards within the team.

Tackling Time Wasters
Time Management

Time wasters in the form of interruptions and distractions are an inherent part of working with others. Good time management requires effective teamwork so that we use our own time well while helping others use theirs to advantage. Invest some energy in analyzing how your time is used interacting with others and in discussing how to create time management solutions that benefit everyone.

Handle Interruptions

- Analyze the interruptions.

  - Note repeated instances as to who is involved, when the interruptions occur, how long they last, and what they are about.

  - Look for patterns among the interruptions and try to be proactive in solving the problem.

- Keep the interruption brief.

  - Work during hours of normal break time for others.

  - Gently encourage visitors to get to the point quickly.

- Stand up, inquire as to the reason for the visit, and remain standing while you talk.

- Go to other people's offices when they need to see you.

- Cluster things together.

  - Use notebook, file folder, or tray to bunch various items for a single discussion.

  - Schedule regular meetings with key people to address routine matters.

  - Encourage others to set appointments with you rather than drop by.

- Tame the telephone.

  - Plan your calls before you dial by asking yourself the following questions: Why am I calling? What do I want to say? How much time will I need for the call?

  - Be concise, give complete information, and avoid small talk.

  - Arrange telephone appointments to avoid "phone tag."

  - Consider alternative ways to contact people (for example, fax, e-mail, voice mail).

- Trim telephone tag.

  - Ask the person when is the best time to call.

  - If the person is unavailable, ask if someone else can help.

  - Leave a complete message (who you are, why you are calling, when and where you can be reached, and any information you need to obtain).

- Curb socializing.

  - Avoid congregating in areas that cause a distraction to others.

  - Arrange work space to eliminate casual socializing.

Reduce Distractions

- Reduce surrounding noise levels.

  - Lower ringer volume on phones and use blinking lights instead of bells or buzzers.

  - Place printers, copiers, noisy equipment, and coffee machines in separate rooms.

  - Use white noise in the background to mask ordinary office noises.

- Arrange the environment.

  - Arrange your furniture so that you prevent voices from carrying into your work space.

  - Analyze the floor plan and arrange it so that people who must interact often are placed close together.

  - If necessary, find a place to hide when you need quiet time or complete concentration.

- Stop mental procrastination.

  - Don't look for something to interrupt you in order to avoid working on a project.

  - Become involved in your work, and you will take less notice of the various distractions around you.

section
FOUR

Problem Solving

Problem solving plays a significant role in the customer service process. Although there are a variety of approaches, the key to finding a proper solution generally comes from extensive investigation and observation. A search for patterns leads to logical conclusions, but people need to remain flexible enough to allow for changes in the thinking model as new information is collected. Therefore, good service involves creative, "outside-the-box" thinking. Those who give the best service do so by offering customers options, alternatives, and new ways of doing things.

To acquire this logical yet creative kind of problem-solving mind-set, service representatives must recognize when things are wrong and then do something to change them. This requires remaining open to recommendations and being flexible when particular circumstances may require deviations from policy in order to meet customer needs. The key to accomplishing this type of problem solving involves comprehending the entire scope of the problem before developing a solution for it.

Showing genuine interest in the needs or problems of a customer is essential to building a successful partnering relationship. By treating each client equitably, but not necessarily uniformly, and looking for as many alternatives to the solution as possible, a representative will find it easier to match what the customer wants to what he or she can offer. What solves a problem for one customer doesn't necessarily solve a similar problem for another customer. However, a service provider must not create overly disparate solutions for various customers, or a particular client may feel slighted. As the employee works to create the solution, he or she should speak in positive terms and express the benefits of the solution to the customer.

Because the problem-solving process may result in differing ideas and viewpoints, conflict can be a natural outcome. Differences often can be used to provide the necessary boost to creative problem solving, but if they cannot be resolved, conflict becomes a negative influence. Conflict management requires flexibility and constant evaluation to be truly effective, and communication plays a significant role in the overall process.

Another part of the problem-solving process involves negotiation. Successful negotiation satisfies as much as possible the legitimate interests of all parties; that is, all parties find the terms to be an agreeable solution, judged by objective standards. At the same time, a good working relationship has to be maintained. Service providers must approach negotiation with an open mind and avoid preconceived perceptions. In this way, they can negotiate solutions that are satisfying to the customer and still meet company policies.

Most important, service providers must include personal communications with customers as a key part of the problem-solving strategy. Responding personally creates an opportunity for dialogue with customers—an opportunity to listen, ask questions, explain, apologize, and achieve closure.

In the pursuit of excellence, service providers must use superior problem-solving skills to understand all aspects of the specific problem and to search for solutions that are acceptable. This means examining underlying issues and taking time to prevent problems in the future. A problem-solving attitude doesn't necessarily mean looking at everything as a problem, but rather thinking about what is happening, what outcomes are expected, and what alternatives might be. This mind-set is an active and creative one that keeps the employee alert and involved in any interaction.

Comic Relief

Analyzing Problem Situations

Goal   To practice using a structured approach to problem solving. Participants will solve a character's problem by analyzing the situation, identifying possible solutions, and selecting the best resolution.

Time Required   Approximately 45 minutes to 1 hour

Group Size   Subgroups of three to five persons each, with a maximum of thirty participants

Materials

- One copy of the Comic Relief Worksheet and a pencil for each participant

- A video clip from a TV cartoon or situational comedy series that involves a dilemma for one of its characters without showing the resolution

- VCR and monitor

● ●

PROCESS

1. Introduce the session by stating that customers expect service representatives to come up with workable solutions to a variety of problems. This activity is designed to help the participants practice using a structured approach to effective problem solving.

2. Form subgroups of three to five persons each.

3. Distribute one copy of the worksheet and a pencil to each subgroup.

4. Explain that the participants will be viewing a video clip that presents a dilemma for one of its characters. Referring to the worksheet, tell the groups that they will have 20 minutes to attempt to solve the character's problem by following the IDEA problem-solving process: (1) Identify the problem by analyzing it, (2) Diagnose the factors and forces causing the problem, (3) Explore all the possible ways in which the problem might be solved, and (4) Apply the best solution to the problem and state the reason(s) why it was chosen.

5. Allow approximately 20 minutes for the groups to complete the task, giving a 2-minute warning before time expires.

6. Ask each subgroup in turn to describe how they used the structured four-step approach to arrive at the best solution for solving the character's problem.

7. Facilitate a large group discussion by asking the following questions:

   • How difficult was it to analyze the situation and formulate a problem statement? Why?

   • Why is it important to have a clear understanding of the entire issue before developing a solution for it?

   • What role does perception play in solving problems?

   • Why does problem solving rely on both logical and creative thinking?

   • What specific things can be done to increase creative thinking during the problem-solving process?

   • How does this activity relate to solving problems for your own customers?

VARIATION

If you are working with a small group of participants (ten or fewer), use the video clip or a comic series from the newspaper. If using a printed comic, enlarge it and mount on tag board for display (or create an overhead transparency). Use a flip chart to duplicate the information from the worksheet and have the entire group work together to complete the exercise.

COMIC RELIEF WORKSHEET

IDENTIFY: What is the problem?

DIAGNOSE: What is causing the problem?

EXPLORE: What are the possible solutions?

APPLY: What is the best solution and why?

Dialing Dilemma
Telephone Logic Problem

Goal To discuss the process of logical problem solving and its implications for customer situations. Participants will solve a number sequencing problem using instructions given on an "automated telephone system" grid.

Time Required Approximately 20 to 30 minutes

Group Size Subgroups of two or three persons each

Materials

● One copy of the Dialing Dilemma Worksheet and a pencil for each person

● Blank flip-chart sheet and a felt-tipped marker for recording results

● Prepared flip chart with the following answer sequence: 1, 2, 5, 8, 3, 7, 6, 5, 8, 4, 9, 6, #, 3, 0

● Masking tape to post prepared flip chart

● Timer or clock

• •

PROCESS

1. Prior to the session, prepare a flip chart with the answer sequence, and post the sheet in a way that keeps the answers hidden from view.

2. At the session, explain to the participants that they will be working in groups to solve a problem that involves a sequence of events.

3. Form subgroups of two or three persons each.

4. Distribute a copy of the worksheet and a pencil to each participant. Read aloud the directions at the top of the page.

5. Tell the groups that they will have 5 minutes in which to determine the correct sequencing by following the directions given on the worksheet.

6. Time the activity for 5 minutes and then signal for the groups to stop working.

7. Ask each group to report its sequence, recording the results on a blank flip-chart sheet.

8. Reveal the correct answer on the prepared flip chart: 1, 2, 5, 8, 3, 7, 6, 5, 8, 4, 9, 6, #, 3, 0. Determine which groups solved the problem correctly.

9. Explain that an essential part of problem solving involves the determination of a series of logical steps to obtain a solution and the actual execution of the steps outlined in your plan.

10. Facilitate a large group discussion based on the following questions:

    • How did you feel during this exercise? What factors contributed to your reaction?

    • How can we relate this exercise to the experience of a customer using a complicated or poorly designed automated telephone system?

    • What reactions might the customer have?

    • How could this affect a service representative's ability to solve a customer's problem?

    • Why does the logical problem-solving process support both the task and the relationship aspects of the customer-based interaction?

VARIATION

For participants from the same organization, follow up with an additional exercise that attempts to re-create the actual phone path of the company. Ask the participants to determine its strengths and weaknesses, then ask for ways to improve the system.

DIALING DILEMMA WORKSHEET

Directions: You are a customer trying to reach the ABC Company using their new automated telephone system. Begin in the first panel and follow the directions it gives. You will find yourself jumping from panel to panel as you are instructed to press the next key. Determine the proper answer sequence by writing down the keys you press each time you proceed to the next one. Try to make contact with your service representative by completing the correct sequence.

1	2 ABC	3 DEF
Thank you for calling the ABC Company automated telephone system. If you wish to proceed, press 2 now or press * to end this call.	To continue, press 5 and listen. If the instructions at 5 would cause you to press 9, ignore them and press 8. If they would cause you to press 8, ignore them and press 9.	Press the key directly to the left of the one you pressed just before this one.
4 GHI	**5 JKL**	**6 MNO**
If at any time you are instructed to press *, do not. Instead press the key at the top of the column where the key containing the instructions is located. Press 9 now.	If the last key you pressed was in the same column as this one, press 9 now. If not, press 8 now.	If the sum of the last three keys you pressed before the 6 equals 18, press 5 now. If the sum is 20, press 1 now. If it is neither, press # now.
7 PQRS	**8 TUV**	**9 WXYZ**
If the letters on the last four keys you pressed before the 7 could spell "melt," press 4. If they could spell "clue," press 6 now. If neither, press #.	If you have pressed five keys or fewer, press 3 now. If six or more keys, press 4 now.	Press 6 to continue. If the instructions at 6 would cause you to press 1, ignore them and press #. If they would cause you to press 3, press * instead.
*	**0 OPER**	**#**
Good-bye *(click)*	Hello, ABC Company. May I help you?	Press * now.

Answer Sequence:

It's All in How You Look at It

Problem Interpretation

Goal

To explore how the articulation and interpretation of a problem affect the solution. The participants will develop solutions to two problems, the first stated in slightly varying terms and the second stated in exact terms.

Time Required

Approximately 30 to 45 minutes

Group Size

Five subgroups of three to five persons each

Materials

- Ten index cards and a felt-tipped pen to create problem cards (see Process section)

- One sheet of paper and a pencil for each person

PROCESS

1. Prior to the session, prepare two sets of index cards as directed below.

    Set A: Create one card for each statement (or create an alternate version, writing each problem in five different ways by changing only one word each time):

    Design a waterproof container.

    Design a watertight container.

    Design a water-resistant container.

    Design a leakproof container.

    Design a water-repellant container.

    Set B: Create five separate cards with the following statement on each: Design a flotation device.

2. At the session, explain that the participants will be working together in groups to practice their problem-solving skills.

3. Form subgroups of three to five persons each. Using the Set A cards, distribute one index card to each subgroup. Provide each participant with paper and a pencil for notes.

4. Explain that the groups will have 5 minutes to develop the best possible solution.

5. Stop the groups after approximately 5 minutes. Have each group in turn read the problem statement and present the solution. Compare the different solutions.

6. Ask the following questions:

    *   Although the descriptive words were similar in all the problem statements, did the subtle differences affect the solutions? Why or why not?

    *   In what ways were the solutions the same? Different?

    *   How does the interpretation and articulation of a problem affect the eventual solution?

7. Explain that the groups will now have 5 minutes to develop a solution to another problem. Using the Set B cards, distribute one index card to each group.

8. Stop the groups after approximately 5 minutes. Explaining that all the groups had the same problem statement this time, have each group in turn present its solution. Compare the different solutions.

9. Facilitate a large group discussion by asking the following questions:

   • Were there just as many different solutions when groups had the exact same problem statement as when groups had altered statements?

   • How do subtle differences in interpreting problems affect solutions in the workplace?

   • How can we use this information to improve our ability to solve problems in the workplace?

Medical Breakthrough
Logical Problem Analysis

Goal   To examine the process of logical analysis in solving problems. Participants will work in groups to solve a logic problem.

Time Required   Approximately 45 minutes to 1 hour

Group Size   Subgroups of three or four persons each

Materials

- One copy of the Medical Breakthrough Worksheet and a pencil for each participant

- One copy of the Medical Breakthrough Solution Sheet for each participant

- Two flip-chart newsprint sheets and a felt-tipped marker for recording data

- Masking tape for posting newsprint sheets

- Timer or clock

PROCESS

1. Prior to the session, become familiar with the information provided on the solution sheet so that you can clarify any questions from the participants.

2. Form subgroups of three or four persons each.

3. Distribute one copy of the worksheet and a pencil to each participant.

4. Explain that members of the subgroups are to work together to solve the logic problem presented. As each group completes the task, one representative is to stand so that the completion time can be recorded.

5. Record the completion time for each group on a newsprint sheet. Stop the activity after approximately 20 minutes if not all groups have finished. Post the newsprint sheet.

6. Obtain the solution information from each subgroup and record the answers on a blank newsprint sheet.

7. Distribute one copy of the solution sheet to each participant. Read aloud the answer and then allow several minutes for the groups to read and discuss the answers. Clarify any information as necessary.

8. Ask the following questions:

    -   What was your group's approach to solving this problem?

    -   Was this process effective? Why or why not?

9. Explain that logic problems involve using the information provided, whether directly or indirectly. Because the information is often sketchy or irrelevant, it is necessary to first draw some inferences by analyzing basic facts. The resulting conclusions enable us to collect additional data in order to arrive at a final solution.

10. Facilitate a large group discussion by asking the following questions:

    -   What factors affected your ability to solve the problem?

    -   What information was not necessary in solving the problem? *(color of rooms)* How does extraneous information affect one's ability to solve problems effectively?

    -   How did time pressure affect your problem-solving skills? How does this relate to solving problems on the job?

- What participant roles (for example, leader, recorder, negotiator, and so forth) emerged during the activity?

- How did these roles help the problem-solving process? How did they hinder it?

- How can you relate your experience with this activity to situations in your workplace?

- What are some ways in which you can improve your process of analyzing and solving problems on the job?

MEDICAL BREAKTHROUGH WORKSHEET

Problem

Five individual patients have been admitted to the hospital. Each person has only one disease, each different from the others. Each one occupies a separate room, numbered from 101 to 105.

Read the information and answer the questions.

1. The person with asthma is in Room 101.

2. Mr. Jones has heart disease.

3. Ms. Green is in Room 105.

4. Ms. Smith has tuberculosis.

5. The patient with mononucleosis is in Room 104.

6. Each room is painted a different color.

7. Mr. White is in Room 101.

8. One of the patients, other than Ms. Anderson, has gallbladder disease.

What disease does Ms. Anderson have? _____

What room is she located in? _____

MEDICAL BREAKTHROUGH SOLUTION SHEET

Solution

Ms. Anderson has mononucleosis, and she is in Room 104.

To solve this problem, you can set up a matrix with the names of the patients and the room numbers listed. Then read through the list of statements. In three cases, we find out which patient is in which room; this information allows us to place the word "YES" in three locations in the matrix and to eliminate the other rooms and people in these columns and rows from the "still uncertain" list. (Eliminated items are indicated by an X.)

We also can note the disease where appropriate. Because three patients have identified diseases and the person with gallbladder disease is not Anderson, we can surmise that Green has gallbladder disease. Jones has heart disease and cannot be the patient with mononucleosis in Room 104, so he must be in Room 103. Therefore, Ms. Anderson must be the patient with mononucleosis in Room 104.

	Asthma		Mono		
	101	102	103	104	105
ANDERSON	X	X	X	√	X
JONES *Heart disease*	X	X	?	X	X
GREEN *Gallbladder?*	X	X	X	X	YES
SMITH *Tuberculosis*	X	YES	X	X	X
WHITE *Gallbladder?*	YES	X	X	X	X

Miss Interpretation

Problem Interpretation

Goal   To examine how the interpretation of a problem affects the eventual solution. Participants will follow a general instruction that can be interpreted in various ways.

Time Required   Approximately 15 to 20 minutes

Group Size   Unlimited number of individual participants

Materials

● One sheet of paper of the same size for each person

● ●

PROCESS

1. Introduce the session by stating that solving a problem requires the understanding of the entire scope of the problem.

2. Distribute one sheet of paper to each person.

3. Give the following instruction and do not elaborate on how to accomplish the task: "Fold a piece of paper eight times."

4. Allow a few minutes for completing the task. Observe the various ways in which the participants carry out the instruction. (*Note:* The results of this exercise may be dramatic, including the complaint that it is impossible to perform. If a participant tries to fold the paper in half eight times without unfolding it, it will almost always result in failure.)

5. Ask the following questions:

   • Were you successful in completing the task? Why or why not?

   • Did you interpret the instructions by folding the paper in half eight times in sequence, or did you use a different solution?

   • Why is it easy to misinterpret a problem?

6. Explain that the interpretation of a problem can affect the eventual solution. The first step in solving a problem is recognizing that the problem exists. Next, the problem must be interpreted. Differences in interpretation can be obvious or subtle.

7. Ask the following questions:

   • What are some examples of statements that would not be misinterpreted?

   • How can the misinterpretation of a problem actually enhance our ability to develop an effective solution? *(Looking at things in nontraditional ways can result in finding creative solutions that may have been overlooked otherwise.)*

Nominally Speaking
Nominal Group Technique

Goal   To increase creativity and participation in problem-solving sessions using the Nominal Group Technique. Participants will contribute perceptions, expertise, and experience to define critical issues for a stated problem.

Time Required   Approximately 1 to 1½ hours

Group Size   Five to twelve participants

Materials

- One Nominally Speaking Worksheet and a pencil for each participant

- Twenty index cards for each participant

- A flip chart and felt-tipped marker for recording

● ●

PROCESS

1. Introduce the session by explaining that participants will be using one form of the Nominal Group Technique to focus on defining a problem by evaluating possible solutions.

2. Distribute the worksheet to each participant. Review the problem statement listed on the sheet (or provide another one for the participants).

3. Allow approximately 10 minutes for completion of the form and then stop work.

4. Allow participants to take turns presenting ideas; record these on a flip chart. There should be no discussion or comments made regarding the ideas at this time. Allow participants to contribute any new ideas that may have been inspired by previously stated ones.

5. Number each item and have participants clarify any questions that others have about any of their ideas. Do not condense or categorize ideas.

6. Distribute ten index cards to each participant. Ask each person to select the top ten ideas from the list that they feel are critical to solving the problem and then to rank the cards from 1 to 10 in order of importance, with 1 being the most important and 10 being the least important.

7. Allow approximately 10 minutes for completion, giving a 2-minute warning before time expires.

8. Collect all the cards and tabulate the results on a flip chart. During this phase, ask the participants to briefly discuss their ideas. When all items have been recorded, lead a brief discussion of each item.

9. Distribute ten additional index cards to each participant and ask them to choose the ten most important ideas. The final step is to rank these ten ideas in order of importance, with 1 being the most important and 10 being the least important.

10. Allow approximately 10 minutes for completion, giving a 2-minute warning before time expires.

11. Ask each member to assign a value of 100 to the highest-priority item and a value of 0 to 100 for each of the remaining nine items to indicate relative differences in importance.

12. Allow approximately 5 minutes, giving a 1-minute warning before time expires. Collect and tally the new rankings and ratings (0–100 for each).

13. Explain that the rankings constitute the most favored group actions for dealing with the problem that was the focus of the exercise.

14. Lead a discussion about the entire experience by asking the following questions:

- How would you describe your understanding of the issues affecting the problem before we used this Nominal Group Technique? After the technique was used?

- How was creativity increased through this process?

- What kinds of problems that we typically face as a team might be candidates for this technique?

- What did you like about using this technique? Dislike?

- What are some of the advantages and disadvantages to using this technique for solving problems in the workplace?

NOMINALLY SPEAKING WORKSHEET

Problem: How would you compile and produce an informational brochure about your organization?

List all facts and resources needed to solve the problem. Do not discuss this task with anyone else. Take approximately 10 minutes to work silently and independently.

Role It Out
Situational Role Play

Goal   To practice effective problem solving in terms of task and relationship components. Participants will role-play the parts of employee, customer, and observer in a variety of problem situations.

Time Required   Approximately 1 hour

Group Size   Subgroups of three persons each

Materials

- One copy of the Role It Out Information Sheet and the Role It Out Situations Sheet for each participant

- One copy of the Role It Out Recommended Actions Sheet for each subgroup, cut into slips

- One blank sheet of paper and a pencil for each participant

- Clock or timer

• •

PROCESS

1. Prior to the session, cut each Role It Out Recommended Actions Sheet into three separate slips.

2. Introduce the session by stating that problem solving generally requires the ability to maintain a good relationship with the customer as well as to perform a task that helps resolve the problem. These two components are equally important to providing quality service. This activity is designed to help the participants practice their problem-solving skills in both areas.

3. Form subgroups of three persons each. Provide a number designation to each member of a group.

4. Distribute one copy each of the information sheet and the situations sheet, as well as a blank sheet of paper and a pencil to each participant.

5. Explain that three rounds of role play will be conducted, with each group member having the opportunity to practice the roles of employee, customer, and observer. Review the information sheet. Note that the blank paper is to be used by the observer for taking notes.

6. Announce the beginning of Round 1 using Situation #1. Time the activity for 10 minutes, giving a 2-minute warning before time expires.

7. Explain that there are some basic task actions that the employee should take to provide resolution of the problems. Distribute the Recommended Action Sheet slip for Situation #1 to each subgroup. Allow several minutes for discussion and then obtain feedback on the employee role from each subgroup.

8. Repeat steps 6 and 7 for Round 2 with Situation #2 and then for Round 3 with Situation #3.

9. Facilitate a large group discussion by asking the following questions:

   • How effectively do you support both the task and relationship aspects of your customer interactions?

   • What guidelines do you use to determine how well you meet your customers' needs?

   • What aspects of telephone complaints might present unique challenges to solving problems? What about face-to-face encounters?

   • What specific actions can you take to improve the way in which you solve customer problems?

ROLE IT OUT INFORMATION SHEET

Practice Rounds

1. Each round lasts 10 minutes. The facilitator will announce the beginning and ending times.

2. The roles switch and a new situation is used for each round:

    Round 1: Member 1 is the employee, Member 2 is the customer, Member 3 is the observer

    Round 2: Member 2 is the employee, Member 3 is the customer, Member 1 is the observer

    Round 3: Member 3 is the employee, Member 1 is the customer, Member 2 is the observer

3. After the practice, each member reports on what went well in resolving the problem and satisfying the customer and then on what could have been done differently. Have participants report in the following order: first the employee, next the customer, and finally the observer.

4. The next section lists guidelines that should be used to determine the effectiveness of the service interaction.

Solving the Problem While Saving the Relationship

To maintain the relationship component of the transaction, you should always express your understanding of the situation:

*   Focus on recognizing the customer's point of view and empathize.

*   Be direct and forthright about the situation.

*   Approach the situation with a positive attitude and tone.

*   Do not place blame or make excuses.

To maintain the task component, specify what you plan to do to resolve the situation:

*   Deal with the unique aspects of each situation.

*   Explain why you are doing something.

*   Explain how the customer will benefit from the solution.

*   Give dates and deadlines.

*   Make amends and try to find ways to "go the extra mile."

*   Follow up and keep the customer informed of any progress.

ROLE IT OUT SITUATIONS SHEET

Situation #1

Employee: This is the third time you have come to the customer's residence to repair a product that your company recently began selling. The problems always seem to be related to one particular component that apparently was not properly assembled at the manufacturing plant.

Customer: You have had to take time off from work each time a service call was necessary. You are becoming increasingly annoyed with the continuing problem. You are agitated as soon as the service representative arrives.

Situation #2

Employee: You manage a large supply store, and you are answering a telephone call regarding a special order that the customer placed ten days ago. Half of the order was delivered, but the other half has been misplaced.

Customer: You have had to make several calls and trips to the store to try to locate your order. You are a longtime customer of the store, and you have not encountered problems before, but you are losing patience because you need the supplies immediately.

Situation #3

Employee: A customer has called on the telephone with a complaint, and you are the third person to whom the caller has been referred.

Customer: You are very angry because you are convinced that the problem was caused by the company, and no one seems to want to take responsibility for solving the problem.

ROLE IT OUT RECOMMENDED ACTIONS SHEET

Situation #1

Explain that you will repair the product and that you will notify your manager of the recurring problem. Document the interaction and advise your manager immediately about the situation. Within a few days, you should check with the manager to find out your company's policy for handling the recurring problem and/or the manufacturer's response. Make a follow-up telephone call to the customer to determine if there are any continuing problems and to give an update on any further actions that are being taken in regard to the product's continued performance.

Situation #2

The customer has been inconvenienced because of mistakes made by your company, and you may potentially lose his or her business. First make sure that the customer receives the order by having it delivered directly. Provide some additional value to the customer to make up for the problem and to show that the customer's business is important; for example, provide a certificate worth some amount for purchase at the store.

Situation #3

Do not refer the customer on to anyone else and do not make the customer wait. Listen carefully to the details of the problem, summarize them, and ask what solution the customer would find satisfactory. If you can help, do so. If you cannot help or if you need to collect more information, give the customer your name and phone number and tell the customer what you must do (pass the problem to someone else, get more information, and so forth). Tell the customer that he or she will be contacted by a specific time, then pass the details to or obtain the information from the proper person in the company. You should call the customer by the time indicated, even if you have turned the problem over to someone else. You are not personally removed from the problem until the customer is satisfied.

Sensible Solutions

Alternative Solutions

Goal
To identify customer service problem situations and develop possible solutions to them. Participants will use personal experiences to develop alternative solutions to customer problems.

Time Required
45 minutes to 1 hour

Group Size
Subgroups of three to five persons each, with a maximum of twenty-five participants

Materials

- One 5" × 8" index card and a pencil for each subgroup

- One newsprint sheet and a felt-tipped marker for each subgroup

- Masking tape for posting newsprint sheets

● ●

PROCESS

1. Form subgroups of three to five participants each.

2. Distribute one index card and a pencil to each subgroup.

3. Direct each subgroup to identify one common service situation that involves a customer complaint or problem. One member of the group is to briefly describe the situation on the index card provided. Allow approximately 5 minutes for group work.

4. Collect the index cards from the groups and shuffle them. Distribute one situation card to each subgroup.

5. Distribute one newsprint sheet and a felt-tipped marker to each subgroup.

6. Explain that the groups will have approximately 15 minutes to discuss the service situation presented on the card and identify all the possible solutions to resolving the complaint or problem. The suggestions are to be recorded on the newsprint sheet provided.

7. After approximately 15 minutes, stop the groups and have them post their newsprint sheets.

8. Ask each subgroup in turn to identify its problem situation and the possible solutions. After each presentation, invite the other participants to comment on the solutions or offer additional ones.

9. Facilitate a large group discussion based on the following questions:

   • How effective were the proposed solutions to the various problems? What made them effective?

   • Did working as a group help or hinder the problem-solving process? Why?

   • What internal factors in the workplace affect the selection of a customer service solution? What external factors are involved? How effective are the solutions? Why?

   • What can be done to facilitate the problem-solving process in your current work environment?

Breaking Barriers
Obstacles to Problem Solving

When the caveman encountered a charging animal, he had to decide quickly whether he was in danger or not. Those who made the right decision survived. Today, our decisions may not always cost us our lives, but bad choices often cause mistakes that can lead to bigger problems.

Directions: On a scale of 1 (never) to 5 (always), rate how often you encounter the following obstacles to solving problems in general. After you have rated all of them, check the solutions column for suggested ways to overcome these barriers and identify those pertinent to you.

Rating	Barrier to Problem Solving	Solution
	Lacking clarity when stating the problem *(Example: Employees must be unhappy since there is a high turnover rate.)*	State what, why, who, when, where, and how much. Avoid wording that will dictate the solution.
	Accepting the first information you get as being correct *(Example: You take the side of the first person who tells you about a conflict situation.)*	Question everything you hear and be skeptical of about half of what you see.
	Being unable to verify if information is correct *(Example: Employees complain that supplies are being stolen.)*	Be skeptical about any information. Make sure to double-check: Is what you hear really "fact" or only "opinion"?
	Rejecting information that contradicts what you think you already know *(Example: If you believe you lack creativity, you won't try to be creative.)*	Decide that what you "know" is either conditioning or just a first impression. It's all right to think differently.
	Failing to see how causes lead to effects *(Example: You don't see how your job affects the company's bottom-line results.)*	Reexamine your assumptions about what leads to what.
	Viewing similar things as being identical *(Example: You think all American products are the best.)*	When things look alike, learn more about them. The more you learn, the better you can distinguish them.
	Giving in to the pressure to conform *(Example: "Everyone does it that way.")*	Examine why this idea prevails. Monitor closely any calculated risks you choose to take.
	Thinking of the world in terms of the past and not of the present *(Example: People only work weekdays from 9 to 5.)*	Assume that your knowledge base can become obsolete over time, and do what you can to update it.

Plans for Improvement

Creativity Quotient

Self-Assessment

A spark of creativity can help service representatives find resourceful solutions to customer problems as well as generate ideas to improve the way in which they perform their jobs in general.

Directions: Respond to each of the following statements in terms of how you would act in most situations. Be honest! Use your score to think about your creativity potential in general and then look for specific ways to open up your creativity.

5 = Always   4 = Often   3 = Sometimes   2 = Seldom   1 = Never

1. I openly and freely exchange ideas with others.   5 4 3 2 1

2. I value "thinking time" in addition to doing things.   5 4 3 2 1

3. I curtail evaluation and judgment as I generate ideas.   5 4 3 2 1

4. I avoid quick, negative criticism of new ideas.   5 4 3 2 1

5. I view the positive points of a new suggestion first.   5 4 3 2 1

6. I use analogies and metaphors to help produce novel ideas.   5 4 3 2 1

7. I look for creative ideas before forming logical, workable solutions.   5 4 3 2 1

8. I define problems in various ways before looking for solutions.   5 4 3 2 1

9. I am confident of my ability to produce valuable ideas and
   solutions.   5 4 3 2 1

10. I stay up-to-date and stimulated by attending seminars, taking
    classes, and the like.   5 4 3 2 1

11. I immerse myself in the challenge of the work.   5 4 3 2 1

12. I seek to learn from my mistakes.   5 4 3 2 1

13. I volunteer for assignments outside the scope of my position.   5 4 3 2 1

14. I work for self-satisfaction as well as necessity.   5 4 3 2 1

15. I feel secure and stable in my current position.   5 4 3 2 1

Total: _____

Scoring:

53–60   Outstanding

45–52   Adequate

36–44   Needs work

35 and below   Inhibited

Actions for Increasing Your Creativity Potential

To the Facilitator   After completion of the rating forms, form small groups to discuss some of the actions identified by individuals and then conduct a large group discussion regarding specific actions that the group as a whole can take to improve creativity on the job.

A CAP-ital Idea
Creative Action Planning

Leader

It is important to encourage service representatives to approach problem solving from different perspectives. A team problem-solving session that encourages members to generate a variety of solutions can spark creative responses. A creative problem-solving approach helps individuals acquire a broad, encompassing outlook that will aid them in meeting the needs of both internal and external clients.

ACTION

Solicit new and different ideas from the customer service team by implementing a Creative Action Planning (CAP) session. This brief meeting (approximately 15 minutes) should have a single agenda item, which is to quickly generate ideas around an immediate business issue.

1. Select and confirm a single issue.

2. Give each person a pad of large self-stick notes and have him or her spend 5 minutes generating ideas independently (one idea per sheet).

3. Ask each team member to present his or her ideas by putting the notes on the wall (or flip chart).

4. With the group as a whole, prioritize or integrate these ideas, creating Plan A, Plan B, and Plan C.

Feelings Check-In
Conflict Reaction Assessment

Leader

Oftentimes individuals must meet together as a group to discuss issues, develop ideas, and solve problems. In these situations, there inevitably will be differences in needs, objectives, values, and expectations. There also may be differences in perceiving motives, words, actions, and circumstances. Healthy conflict helps in the exploration of new ideas, but when people avoid conflict or choose sides, animosities can develop, communication breaks down, trust and mutual support deteriorate, and hostilities may result. It is important to be aware of the feelings of individual group members so that any conflict can be dealt with in a constructive manner.

● ●

ACTION

During a group meeting where controversial topics are discussed or when several different ideas and opinions are being expressed, stop and take the time to gauge the overall reactions of the group to avoid unresolved conflict and move toward problem resolution.

1. Distribute a felt-tipped marker and 5" × 8" index card to each person.

2. Ask each person to write on the card in large letters one word that describes how he or she is feeling at that moment.

3. Ask everyone to hold up his or her card and to look at the variety of responses.

4. Point out how rare it is for different people to bring the same feelings to an experience or situation.

5. Invite individuals to share why they wrote down the words that they did.

6. Ask for suggestions on how the group can move toward constructively solving the problem.

Share to Be Aware
Interdepartmental Problem Solving

Leader

No one should underestimate the power of internal customers. Employees need to understand both how various organizational departments fit into the larger picture and the processes that make those departments interconnected units. Many problems can arise simply from misunderstandings about the functions and responsibilities of other departments. This lack of information also may result in communication breakdowns as well as a failure to make improvements in processes and products. By holding interdepartmental information-sharing sessions on a regular basis, you can open the door to strategic problem solving and innovation.

ACTIONS

Invite representatives from a different organizational department to a meeting with your unit or team.

1. Identify the interactive relationship and structure of both departments in terms of function and responsibilities.

2. Arrange for one representative from each department to make a presentation regarding basic functions, products or services, and special projects.

3. Facilitate a question-and-answer segment.

In conjunction with the presentation meeting or separately, hold a problem-solving session with each department.

1. Identify existing problems that may relate to the functions of both departments.

2. Brainstorm options and determine specific actions that can be taken to alleviate or eliminate the problems.

3. Develop action plans with specific tasks, point persons, and milestones for completion.

Follow up regularly with department liaisons to check progress on the action plans.

Be proactive by facilitating creative problem-solving sessions with representatives from one or more organizational departments.

1. Brainstorm ideas to identify a current trend and then discuss what impact this trend would have on a product or service as it relates to each department.

2. Ask the question, "What is the most unanticipated action that could occur regarding a specific project or with a specific product or service?" and then develop some alternatives to address these unforeseen circumstances.

Crash Control
Conflict Management Styles

Conflict can be defined in many ways—from simple disagreement or disharmony to all-out warfare. Conflict situations can arise on a variety of fronts each day, and there are five basic ways in which individuals tend to resolve issues. Understanding when it is appropriate to use these styles, and the possible negative consequences associated with each, prepares employees to relate to internal and external customers more successfully.

Style	Appropriate Uses	Negative Consequences
Avoiding *Try to solve problem by denying its existence.*	• Issue is trivial, or more pressing issues exist. • Issue seems irrelevant or attributed to other concerns. • There is no chance of satisfying personal goals. • Possible disruption outweighs benefits of resolution. • Process allows people to calm down and regain perspective. • There is a need to gather more information. • Others can resolve issue more effectively.	• Issue may build. • Decisions are made by default. • Person lacks credibility. • Self-esteem is undermined.
Accommodating *Play down differences; surface harmony exists.*	• Harmony and stability are particularly important. • Issue is more important to others. • Person can build "social credits" for later issues. • Person can minimize loss when outmatched and losing. • Avoiding disruption is important. • Continued conflict will damage relationship.	• Person is evading important issues. • Person's influence decreases. • Person can become frustrated if needs are not met. • The best solution may be relinquished. • Self-esteem is undermined.
Competing *Use authority or position to settle issue.*	• Quick, decisive action is vital. • Conflict involves important issues calling for unpopular actions. • Conflict involves issues vital to company welfare. • Others take advantage of non-competitive behavior. • Damaged relationships exist.	• Communication among parties is reduced. • Others feel no sense of commitment. • Future disruptions may occur.

Style	Appropriate Uses	Negative Consequences
Compromising *Each party gives up something to meet midway.*	• Parties with equal power are committed to mutually exclusive goals. • Parties can obtain temporary settlements to complex issues. • Parties can arrive at suitable solutions when significant time pressure exists. • Goals are important, but not worth using more assertive methods.	• No one is fully satisfied. • Process yields a short-term or watered-down solution. • Result can be seen as "selling out."
Collaborating *Recognize abilities, values, expertise of all; each individual position is clear but emphasizes mutual solutions.*	• Combines insights from people with varying viewpoints. • Commitment is increased by incorporating concerns of others. • Process works through emotions interfering with a relationship. • An integrative solution can be found when both sets of concerns are too important to be compromised. • Purpose is to learn.	• Process takes time, abilities, and commitment. • Parties may reach ineffective decisions. • Trust among parties may be compromised.

Source: Adapted from Thomas, K. W. (1977). "Toward multi-dimensional values in teaching: The example of conflict behaviors." *Academy of Management Review, 2,* table 1, p. 487.

Fair Play
Win-Win Negotiation

Successful negotiation with clients requires a realistic framework that helps guide the overall process from beginning to end. The parties should achieve a solution through good communication and with efficient use of time and resources, while maintaining a good working relationship. This means that all parties find the solution agreeable. The outcome should satisfy as much as possible the legitimate interests of all parties, and it should be a creative, "no waste" solution that binds all sides to realistic commitments.

Step 1: Prepare for a Successful Negotiation

- Get the big picture by deciding what is most important.

  What is it that you want to accomplish? Why is it important?

- Decide who is the "right person" with whom to negotiate.

  What is the person's primary style of relating to others and processing information?

  How will your past experiences with this person affect the negotiation process?

- Define the issues on which you already agree.

  What are mutual interests? What is the common ground for starting a negotiation?

- List what you feel to be the real differences in your positions.

- Describe what you feel would be the "ideal" interaction and the desired outcome.

- Determine the outside limits for negotiation from your position.

  What is negotiable and what is not?

- Consider the various options for getting what you want.

  What are the advantages and disadvantages of each option?

  How will the outcome be measured?

Step 2: Develop a Collaborative Relationship

- State your objective to the person and explain your desire to find the best possible solutions so that each of you gets what you really want.

- Ask the other person what he or she wants and why it is important.

- Listen carefully without interrupting or disagreeing in order to understand the other person's position. Ask appropriate questions to gain clarification.

- Accept the other person's right to an opinion and restate the position as you understand it.

- Ask the person to listen to you without interruption as you explain what you want and why.

- Check for mutual understanding of one another's position.

Step 3: Create Win-Win Outcomes

- State your belief that it is possible to find a solution that will satisfy each person's needs.

- Stay rationally focused on the issue being negotiated.

- Be creative at coming up with all the possible ways you can both get what you want.

- Select the best possible option and identify the good points about that idea.

- Problem-solve any objections to move toward acceptance of an idea.

- State the agreed-on solution.

- Express appreciation for the other person's willingness to work toward a solution.

Stage Right
Creative Process

Creative problem solving combines structured (analytical or rational) thinking with imaginative and innovative "repatterning," or looking at things in a totally different way. To solve problems more creatively, try using the creative process described here.

Stage 1: Preparation

Gain foundational information from school, training, reading, traveling, life experiences, and so forth, to scrutinize the need for a solution.

- Finding facts and thinking logically

- Laying the groundwork and learning the background of the problem

- Learning creativity procedures

Stage 2: Concentration

Focus on a specific problem and generate basic ideas.

- Becoming totally absorbed in the problem

- Allowing enough time
- Engaging in basic planning and idea formation

Stage 3: Incubation

Step away from the problem to see hidden associations or connections.

- Taking time for reflection
- Seeking distractions
- Working on other things

Stage 4: Illumination

Open the mind so that new, useful ideas emerge.

- Relaxing
- Combining ideas
- Using resources that help stimulate ideas (for example, art, books, magazines)

Stage 5: Implementation

Make modifications and use the idea.

- Solving practical problems
- Putting ideas into action plans
- Gaining commitment of others

Stage 6: Evaluation

Judge the overall impact of the implemented solution(s).

- Reviewing tangible and intangible outcomes
- Using both objective and subjective measures
- Revising actions as necessary

Quality

Although technical excellence clearly is important, the practical meaning of good service extends far beyond this single component. The ability to provide superior service depends on recognizing what the customer needs and wants. Because the company's ability to provide quality actually starts with the customer, it is from that fundamental basis that service providers must build their approach to exceptional practices. To do so they must bear in mind the unique specific needs of each customer situation in order to present the best possible strategy.

One of the more challenging aspects of quality service is to provide for the uniqueness of each situation. It is important for the success of the organization to remember to treat customers like people and not numbers. This is especially true when dealing with problems because of the emotions that may be part of a customer's concern. These feelings and reactions must be acknowledged and dealt with before moving on to solving the actual problem. By taking the time to know the particulars of each customer's situation, service representatives can become aware of opportunities to "go the extra mile" and exceed the customer's expectations. This means staying attentive to customers, remaining aware of their changing needs, and responding to their demands in a positive and timely manner. Service should be tailored to meet each customer's specific needs to ensure satisfaction and loyalty.

Positive personal performance communicates through actions and words a genuine interest in the needs or problems of the customer, which is essential to building a successful customer relationship. Service providers act as the organization's frontline representatives. It is critical that they focus on *all* aspects of their performance so as to turn service mistakes or customer dissatisfaction into positive experiences that build the company's reputation for quality service.

It is important for service providers to remain flexible and open-minded in order to react to constantly changing technologies and environments. They are often called on to handle difficult situations—customers may disagree with proposed solutions to their problems, or they may demand more than what can be offered. It is the job of the customer service representative to help negotiate solutions that are satisfying to the customer and that meet company policies.

If things are wrong, it is imperative that representatives do whatever they can to correct the problem. Reliable service recovery efforts help communicate to customers that the organization cares, that it is sensitive to customer needs, and that it will stand behind its products or service no matter what. Even when there is no evident problem, it is important to be aware of conditions that contribute to the customer's overall situation. That means looking at all aspects of the big picture and constantly examining these factors for ways to improve service conditions. Soliciting ongoing feedback from customers, both internal as well as external, helps set into motion a system for continuous quality improvement.

Getting the Word Out
Quality Components

Goal   To describe the components of quality customer service. Participants will develop a statement that describes one aspect of quality service for each letter of the word *customer.*

Time Required   Approximately 30 minutes

Group Size   Subgroups of three to five persons each

Materials

- One copy of the Getting the Word Out Worksheet and a pencil for each participant

PROCESS

1. Introduce the session by stating that the ability to provide quality service depends on recognizing what the customer needs and wants. This activity is designed to help the participants get a clearer picture of what is expected of them.

2. Form subgroups of three to five persons each. Ask each group to select a member to record information.

3. Distribute one copy of the worksheet and a pencil to each participant.

4. Explain that the groups are to write one statement describing some aspect of quality customer service for each letter in the word *customer*. For example, the letter *C* might represent the statement, "Complete all transactions by thanking the customer for doing business with the company."

5. Allow approximately 10 minutes for groups to complete the task, giving a 2-minute warning before time expires.

6. Ask each subgroup in turn to read the statements created.

7. Facilitate a large group discussion by asking the following questions:

    • How do you determine the needs of your customers?

    • Are any of the aspects of customer service you listed incompatible with one another? If so, which ones? Why might this occur? If not, what contributes to their compatibility?

    • What are some ways you can implement the service characteristics you described?

GETTING THE WORD OUT WORKSHEET

Directions: For each letter in the word *customer,* write one statement that describes an aspect of providing quality customer service.

C	
U	
S	
T	
O	
M	
E	
R	

Inconvenience Store

Service Strategies

Goal
To develop strategies to facilitate a good customer service experience. Participants will create environments designed to hinder the service experience.

Time Required
Approximately 1 hour

Group Size
Subgroups of four to seven persons each, with a maximum of twenty-five participants

Materials

- A variety of items (such as poster board, boxes, envelopes, felt-tipped markers, ropes, bells, toy phones, and so forth) that can be used as props in a creative skit on customer service

- One sheet of blank paper and a pencil for each participant

- A flip chart and felt-tipped marker for recording information

● ●

PROCESS

1. Prior to the session, place the selected items in a central location in the room.

2. At the session, form subgroups of four to seven persons each. (*Note:* Be sure that each group has sufficient room and privacy to work on a skit.)

3. Distribute one sheet of blank paper and a pencil to each participant.

4. Explain that each subgroup will have 30 minutes to create a 3- to 5-minute skit depicting a face-to-face service environment that *prevents* a customer from having a good experience. Each subgroup will determine which of its members will perform in the skit, but a member of another subgroup will perform as the customer. Groups may use any of the props provided.

5. Allow approximately 30 minutes for group work, giving a 5-minute warning before time expires.

6. Ask each subgroup to select one person to act out the role of a customer. Next, have each subgroup in turn present their skit with one member of another group as the customer.

7. Facilitate a large group discussion by asking the following questions and recording responses on the flip chart, as noted:

    *   For those who played the role of customer, how did you feel during the experience?

    *   What specific actions hindered the customer experience? (Record responses on flip chart.)

    *   What are some examples of the unspoken rules and unspeakable behaviors of service staff? Of customers?

    *   Why is it important to put yourself in the place of the customer when you deal with complaints or concerns?

    *   How do you determine the specific needs of your own clientele?

    *   What are some actions you can take to improve the customer service experience in your workplace? (Record responses on flip chart.)

Like It or Not
Service Analogies

Goal   To explore aspects of customer service through the use of analogies. Participants will develop five statements that link customer service to other concepts.

Time Required   Approximately 30 minutes

Group Size   Up to six subgroups of five to eight persons each

Materials

- One copy of a Like It or Not Worksheet for each participant, with a different version being provided to each subgroup
- A pencil for each participant

● ●

PROCESS

1. Prior to the session, duplicate the worksheet pages and cut each in half to produce two separate worksheets. Prepare enough copies of each worksheet to provide one for each member of a subgroup, while giving a different worksheet version to each subgroup.

2. At the session, explain that analogical thinking helps generate ideas by focusing on similarities between a topic and something completely different. Participants will use this creative approach to look at customer service in a fresh, new way.

3. Form subgroups of five to eight persons each.

4. Distribute one copy of a worksheet and a pencil to each participant, assigning different analogies to each subgroup.

5. Explain that each person is to complete the worksheet by listing three ways in which customer service can be related to the item listed. Individuals will have 5 minutes to complete the assignment.

6. Allow approximately 5 minutes for completion of the task, giving a 1-minute warning before time expires.

7. Explain that members of each subgroup will have approximately 15 minutes to discuss their individual responses. They are to compare answers and look at examples of why these responses were provided. As a final step, each subgroup is to identify the best five responses to report to the larger group.

8. Allow approximately 15 minutes for discussion, giving a 2-minute warning before time expires.

9. Ask each subgroup in turn to report the top five responses selected. After all subgroups have reported, ask for some examples of responses that were not selected for the final list for each analogy.

10. Facilitate a discussion with the whole group by asking the following questions:

    • Were the majority of characteristics positive or negative? Why?

    • What specific issues regarding customer service did these viewpoints address?

    • As a result of this exercise, what new insights did you gain regarding the service you provide?

    • How can you use this information to make the service you provide more effective?

LIKE IT OR NOT WORKSHEET 1

CUSTOMER SERVICE is like a **SCIENCE FICTION NOVEL** because . . .

LIKE IT OR NOT WORKSHEET 2

CUSTOMER SERVICE is like a **SPRING SHOWER** because . . .

LIKE IT OR NOT WORKSHEET 3

CUSTOMER SERVICE is like a **SYMPHONY** because . . .

LIKE IT OR NOT WORKSHEET 4

CUSTOMER SERVICE is like an **ALARM CLOCK** because . . .

LIKE IT OR NOT WORKSHEET 5

CUSTOMER SERVICE is like a **PALM TREE** because . . .

LIKE IT OR NOT WORKSHEET 6

CUSTOMER SERVICE is like an **ELECTRIC FAN** because . . .

Making the Connection
Customer Expectations

Goal
To explore ways in which service representatives meet the needs and expectations of their customers. Participants will generate a list of words that describe aspects of quality customer service from a given word phrase.

Time Required
Approximately 20 to 30 minutes

Group Size
Either an unlimited number of individual participants, or subgroups of three to five persons each

Materials

- One copy of the Making the Connection Worksheet and a pencil for each participant

- Flip chart and felt-tipped marker for facilitator

- Clock or timer

- Prize (optional)

PROCESS

1. Address the group as individual performers, or you may wish to have the participants form subgroups of three to five persons each.

2. Distribute one copy of the worksheet and a pencil to each participant.

3. Explain that each individual (or subgroup) will list as many different words that can be formed from the letters found within the phrase *customer service excellence*. The words should relate to ways in which quality customer service can be provided. To form a word, each letter may be used only as many times as it occurs in the actual phrase. For example, words may only have one *m,* but as many as four *c's.*

4. Allow approximately 5 minutes for completion of the task, then stop the activity.

5. Ask for the words that were formed and how each relates to providing excellent customer service. Record the words on the flip chart. Some possible words include *listen, more, most, excel, restore, custom, receive, nice, silence, client, voice.*

6. *Optional:* Provide a prize to the individual (or subgroup) with the longest list of words.

7. Facilitate a large group discussion based on the following questions:

   • How well do you personally meet your customers' needs? How well does your organization meet their needs? Give situational examples of each.

   • What are the stated values of your organization's service program? How are these values supported?

   • How can you improve your own customer service skills?

   • How can the organization improve its customer service abilities?

MAKING THE CONNECTION WORKSHEET

Directions: Using the letters found in the phrase below, list as many different words as you can that describe aspects of providing quality customer service. To form a word, you may use each letter only as many times as it occurs in the actual phrase; for example, you are allowed only one *m*, but as many as four *c*'s in any individual word.

CUSTOMER SERVICE EXCELLENCE

Overcharged and Underrated
Exceeding Expectations

Goal   To develop strategies for improved service to exceed customer expectations. Participants will view a customer service scenario and critique ways to improve the interaction.

Time Required   Approximately 20 to 30 minutes

Group Size   Eight to twenty individuals

Materials

- Two copies of the Overcharged and Underrated Role-Play Sheet

● ●

PROCESS

1. Ask for two volunteers and provide each with a copy of the role-play sheet. Assign the role of Pat to one volunteer and the role of Casey to the other.

2. Read aloud to the whole group the Roles and Scenario sections of the sheet. Next, have the volunteers read their respective parts from the Script section. Finally, read the Outcome section after the scene has been acted out.

3. Facilitate a large group discussion by asking the following questions:

   • What were your first impressions after seeing this role play?

   • What do you think might be the long-term result of this situation?

   • What would you change about this scene to make it a more successful interaction?

   • Which processes or procedures in your workplace facilitate a successful customer experience? Which ones hinder it?

   • What workplace strategies could be developed to help maintain long-term customer relationships?

OVERCHARGED AND UNDERRATED ROLE-PLAY SHEET

Roles

Pat Harris, national sales manager for the Strider Shoe Corporation, who made arrangements at the Starview Inn for a three-day conference with sixty-five attendees

Casey Wilkens, manager of the Starview Inn and supervisor of a staff of three clerks who handle daily transactions for guests

Scenario

Pat approached the hotel registration desk and asked to talk to someone about being overcharged for hotel services. Casey has arrived at the reception desk to discuss the situation with Pat.

Script

Pat: I really don't understand all of the items on my bill. It is about $900 more than I expected.

Casey: Well, we seldom make an error, but let me review the charges.

Pat: Here's the bill. I don't understand why it includes so many individual room charges.

Casey: *(spoken with a hint of indifference)* My records indicate that sixty-five Strider Shoe Corporation employees stayed with us for three nights. It looks like a large number of them used room service for food and beverages. Frankly, I don't think this bill is out of line.

Pat: I didn't authorize these individual purchases. My boss will be furious if I exceed the budget for this conference by $900!

Casey: *(spoken with a hint of anger in his voice)* Mr. [Ms.] Harris, you arranged for sixty-five Strider employees to register at this hotel. At no time did you request our staff to restrict room service for these people. Do you expect our staff to refuse service to a registered guest?

Pat: Look, this is the first time I've been in charge of a national sales conference for our employees. I simply didn't realize that so many people would use room service.

Casey: *(spoken in a critical tone of voice)* Next time, I would suggest that you discuss this matter with your employees prior to the beginning of the conference.

Pat: I'm really disappointed that I didn't receive any guidance from the hotel when I made the arrangements. I guess I've learned a lot from this experience.

Outcome

Pat turned and walked out of the hotel with a very dejected and unhappy look.

Casey turned to a clerk seated nearby and said, "All sales managers are alike. When it comes to conference planning, they never pay any attention to the important details."

Picture Perfect

Communicating Quality

Goal
To communicate perceptions of quality customer service through printed media. Participants will create an advertisement on customer service using specific words and phrases.

Time Required
Approximately 1 hour

Group Size
Subgroups of four or five persons each, with a maximum of thirty participants

Materials

- Three 3" × 5" index cards and a pencil for each participant

- One poster board sheet and a set of felt-tipped markers in a variety of colors for each subgroup

- Masking tape for posting

• •

PROCESS

1. Form subgroups of four or five persons each.

2. Distribute three index cards and a pencil to each participant.

3. Explain that individuals have 2 minutes to write on each card one word that relates in some way to customer service.

4. Allow approximately 2 minutes for completion of the task.

5. Collect all the cards and shuffle them. Redistribute the cards, providing three to each person.

6. Explain that each group is to examine the cards and choose the five cards with the words that they feel are most often used in relation to customer service in general.

7. Allow approximately 5 minutes for discussion and then collect the extra cards from all groups.

8. Explain that each group will incorporate the selected words into a comprehensive poster advertisement about quality customer service. The groups may use any type of graphics in their advertisements, but the only words they may use are the ones they chose.

9. Distribute one poster board and a set of felt-tipped markers to each subgroup.

10. Allow approximately 20 minutes for completion of the task, giving a 5-minute warning before time expires.

11. Provide the groups with masking tape and direct them to post their advertisements. Have each subgroup make a short presentation on the concept behind its advertisement. (*Optional:* You may wish to leave the posters hanging for the remainder of a training session.)

12. Facilitate a large group discussion by asking the following questions:

    • What common themes regarding customer service do the advertisements share?

    • Were similar words or phrases used? If so, what were they?

    • How clearly did the advertisements actually communicate what the groups wanted to convey?

- How difficult was it to create a concise and accurate message using limited words? Why?

- How is advertising used to influence customers? What role does perception play?

- Given that individual perceptions may differ, what can organizations do to meet specific customer expectations for quality service?

RATER of the Lost Art
Customer Perception of Quality

Goal To examine customer expectations for quality service. Participants will identify examples of five service dimensions and rate their overall degree of importance.

Time Required Approximately 1 hour

Group Size Five subgroups of four or five persons each, with a maximum of twenty-five participants

Materials

- One sheet of blank paper and a pencil for each participant
- One prepared newsprint sheet and tape for posting
- Flip chart and felt-tipped marker for facilitator

● ●

PROCESS

1. Prior to the session, prepare a newsprint sheet with the information shown on the RATER of the Lost Art Information Sheet and post in a prominent location.

2. Introduce the session by referring to the newsprint sheet. Explain that these five dimensions have been found to be critical elements in the perception of the customer in terms of service quality, according to survey results from an ongoing research study conducted by Texas A & M and Duke Universities (Berry, Zeithaml, & Parasuraman, *Sloan Management Review,* Summer 1990, pp. 29—38). Tell the participants that they will be identifying ways in which these dimensions contribute to the overall perception.

3. Form five subgroups of four or five persons each.

4. Distribute one blank sheet of paper and a pencil to each participant. Referring to the flip chart, assign a different service dimension to each subgroup.

5. Tell the groups that they will have approximately 10 minutes to discuss the dimension assigned to each. Each group is to list real-world examples and determine the overall importance of the assigned quality dimension as it feels customers ranked them in the research study, with 1 being most important and 5 being least important.

6. Allow approximately 10 minutes for completion of the task, giving a 1-minute warning before time expires.

7. Refer to the newsprint sheet and ask the groups in turn to provide examples for each dimension. After all the groups have reported on their examples, ask each group to provide the estimated ranking for its dimension within the context of all five and record the number.

8. Reveal the following rankings that were ascertained by the research survey, writing the numbers on the newsprint sheet next to the appropriate words: (1) reliability, (2) responsiveness, (3) assurance, (4) empathy, (5) tangibles.

9. Ask the following questions:

   • How well did your group do in ranking its quality dimension, according to the survey results? Why?

- What role does perception play in satisfying an individual customer's expectations?

10. Explain that the research shows that, foremost, customers expect companies to do what they are supposed to do; they want performance, not empty promises. Customers will not even consider the other four dimensions identified if this basic one is not satisfactory. In order to attain *quality* service, you need to address the other four dimensions.

11. Ask subgroups to discuss the conditions in their own organization that help or hinder the ability to perform satisfactorily on each of these five service dimensions.

12. Allow approximately 15 minutes for discussion, giving a 2-minute warning before time expires.

13. Ask for feedback from the subgroups, recording the responses on a separate flip-chart sheet for each dimension.

14. Facilitate a large group discussion by asking the following questions:

- What actions can individuals take to perform well in terms of accuracy?

- How can service providers best offer empathy to their customers?

- What might the organization do to better meet customer expectations in terms of reliability? responsiveness? tangibles?

RESPONSIVENESS

How quickly things get done

ASSURANCE

Knowledgeable and courteous employees

TANGIBLES

Appearance and convenience of facilities and personnel

EMPATHY

Amount of concern shown to customers

RELIABILITY

Doing what is promised

Right Approach
Service Attitude

Goal   To examine how personal attitude affects situational outcomes for customer service quality. Participants will read a case study regarding customer service attitudes and discuss their personal experiences.

Time Required   Approximately 1 hour

Group Size   Subgroups of three or four persons each, with a maximum of thirty participants

Materials

- One copy of the Right Approach Worksheet for each participant

PROCESS

1. Introduce the session by stating that an attitude can be defined as a relatively strong belief or feeling toward a person, object, idea, or event. Both individual and organizational attitudes can have significant impact on customer service interactions. This activity will provide an opportunity to examine how attitudes influence service outcomes.

2. Form subgroups of three or four persons each.

3. Distribute one copy of the worksheet to each participant.

4. Referring to the worksheet, read aloud the scenario. Tell the subgroups to spend approximately 30 minutes using the questions provided to discuss their own experiences.

5. Allow approximately 30 minutes, giving a 5-minute warning before time expires.

6. Ask each subgroup to provide examples, using the discussion questions from the worksheet.

7. Facilitate a large group discussion by asking the following questions:

    - How are attitudes formed?

    - Are positive attitudes supported by your organization? How is this accomplished?

    - Who are the "Stew Leonards" in your organization? How so?

    - How can you use the insight gained from this activity to provide exceptional customer service?

RIGHT APPROACH WORKSHEET

Scenario

Stew Leonard, the owner of Stew Leonard's, the "world's largest dairy store" (located in Norwalk, Connecticut), credits his ultimate success to a change in attitude that he made shortly after the store opened.

He was standing at the store's entrance when a customer came up and said in an angry voice, "This eggnog is sour." Stew took the half-gallon container, opened it, and took a taste. He then looked the customer in the eye and said, "You're wrong; it's perfect." And to prove that he was right, he added, "We sold over three hundred half-gallons of eggnog this week, and you're the only one who complained." The angry customer demanded her money back and said, "I'm never coming back to this store again!"

That evening, Stew reflected on the incident and came to the conclusion that he had made two huge mistakes. First, he had not listened to the customer, and second, he had humiliated her by saying that three hundred other customers had not complained. He decided that the success of his small store would depend on good customer service that would generate repeat business. He decided to adopt two basic store policies, which have been chiseled into a three-ton rock next to the front door of the store. The simple message reads:

Rule 1: THE CUSTOMER IS ALWAYS RIGHT!

Rule 2: IF THE CUSTOMER IS EVER WRONG, REREAD RULE 1.

Source: Leonard, S. (1988, June 27). Love your customer. *Newsweek.*

Discussion Questions

1. What similar situations have you experienced, either as a customer or as a service provider?

2. How did your personal attitude affect the situation?

3. How did the other person's attitude affect the situation?

4. Did either of you change your attitude during the conversation?

5. What was the end result of this interaction?

Service Link
Creative Analysis of Service

Goal   To creatively examine issues that affect quality customer service. Participants will link disparate words into logical statements about customer service.

Time Required   Approximately 1 hour

Group Size   Subgroups of three or four persons each, with a maximum of thirty participants

Materials

- One sheet of blank paper and a pencil for each participant

- One copy of the Service Link Game Board for each subgroup

- One pair of dice

PROCESS

1. Introduce the session by explaining that participants will be trying to gain a better awareness of customer service issues by linking disparate words together to make logical statements. This creative approach to viewing service elements expands the way in which we provide service to a variety of customers as well as solve potential problems.

2. Form subgroups of three or four persons each. Distribute a sheet of blank paper and a pencil to each participant and one copy of the Service Link Game Board to each subgroup.

3. Explain that you will be rolling dice to provide two numbers that will correspond to the words on the game board. Each participant will write a statement about customer service that links the two words. For example, if numbers 3 and 11 were rolled, the participants would link the words *listening* and *complaint* in a statement—for example, "When there is a *complaint* from a customer, it is important to use active *listening* to understand the details of the situation."

4. Roll one die and announce the number to the groups. Next, roll either one or two dice and announce the number.

5. Allow a few minutes for participants to complete the task. Ask group members to share what each has written and to discuss similarities and differences among their statements.

6. Allow several minutes for discussion and then ask for some examples to be shared with the larger group.

7. Repeat steps 4 through 6 several more times, alternating with rolling one or two dice to obtain the two numbers being provided to the subgroups.

8. Explain that group members now will link three attributes together. Announce three numbers by selecting an appropriate combination of single or double dice rolls. For example, first roll one die, then one die, and finally two dice.

9. If time allows, you may choose to have the subgroups link four attributes together by providing four different numbers as determined by rolls of the dice.

10. Lead a general discussion by asking the following questions:

- How difficult was it for you to create a statement? What factors contributed to this?

- Did individual perceptions within the group differ? If so, in what way?

- What role does perception play in customer service? Give some situational examples.

- What are some ways in which we can use this linking technique to better improve service for our customers?

SERVICE LINK GAME BOARD

1 KNOWLEDGE	2 PERCEPTION	3 LISTENING
4 PROCEDURE	5 SOLUTION	6 QUALITY
7 SATISFACTION	8 CREATIVITY	9 PROFESSIONAL
10 CONCERN	11 COMPLAINT	12 COMMUNICATION

Cream of the Crop
Quality Competencies

Service representatives must posses a wide range of competencies in order to perform their jobs well. These abilities include certain knowledge, skills, and attitudes that support task completion as well as relationship functions. Knowledge includes facts, rules, and concepts necessary to complete a task; skill is the ability to actually execute the task. For example, to answer customer questions, representatives must know certain procedures, but also might need skills to access the computer, analyze the information, or fill out a form. Finally, attitudes are one's personal values and orientations toward the work done. Customer service representatives are expected to have a favorable attitude about working well with other people.

Directions: Examine your overall job performance and respond to each statement below in terms of your ability to respond to customer needs.

5 = Always   4 = Often   3 = Sometimes   2 = Seldom   1 = Never

1. Communication: 5   4   3   2   1

    I use clear communication when keeping my customers informed.

2. Customer sensitivity: 5   4   3   2   1

    I show concern for my customers' feelings and viewpoints.

3. Decisiveness: 5   4   3   2   1

    I make decisions to take action aimed at meeting customer needs.

4. Energy: 5   4   3   2   1

    I portray a high level of vigor, alertness, and attentiveness.

5. Flexibility: 5   4   3   2   1

    I can adapt my style in response to customer needs and personalities.

6. Follow-up: 5   4   3   2   1

    I fulfill promises and commitments in a timely and responsive manner.

7. Initiative: 5   4   3   2   1

    I take action that meets or exceeds customer needs.

8. Integrity: 5   4   3   2   1

    I maintain high ethical standards and act with credibility.

9. Job knowledge: 5   4   3   2   1

    I understand organizational policies, procedures, products, and services.

10. Judgment: 5   4   3   2   1

    I develop effective approaches using available information.

11. Motivation: 5   4   3   2   1

    I derive satisfaction and fulfillment from dealing with customers.

5 = Always   4 = Often   3 = Sometimes   2 = Seldom   1 = Never

12. Persuasiveness: 5   4   3   2   1

   I gain customer acceptance of ideas, products, and services.

13. Planning: 5   4   3   2   1

   I organize my work and prepare for customer interactions.

14. Resilience: 5   4   3   2   1

   I handle problems, unpredictable events, and other job pressures well.

15. Work standards: 5   4   3   2   1

   I establish high personal standards for providing customer service.

Total: _____

Scoring:

   68–75   Excellent service

   60–67   Good service

   51–59   Satisfactory service

   50 and below   Marginal service

Actions you can take for continuous improvement within the next 3 months:

1. _____

2. _____

3. _____

To the Facilitator   Distribute a copy of the assessment to each team member in printed form or by e-mail. Collect the completed evaluations and calculate the average scores for each statement. Conduct a follow-up discussion session to report the results and to explore issues that may be affecting those areas needing improvement. Brainstorm a list of specific actions that should be taken to remedy problems in the work environment that are hindering individuals from providing quality service.

May I Help You?

Telephone Etiquette

In today's widespread service economy, the telephone is one of the most important tools for providing quality service to customers, both internal and external. People call to acquire vital information, provide details, and solve problems. The way in which service providers handle the basics of the call can influence the outcome, both in handling the transaction as well as in the customer's overall perception of the organization.

Directions: Rate yourself on the following statements using the scale below and then look for ways to improve your skills.

5 = Always   4 = Usually   3 = Sometimes   2 = Rarely   1 = Never

1. I answer the call promptly.   5 4 3 2 1

2. I personalize service by using the caller's name.   5 4 3 2 1

3. When it is necessary to place a caller on hold or transfer a call, I ask for permission and wait for an answer.   5 4 3 2 1

4. I tell the customer how long he or she will be on hold and minimize hold time.   5 4 3 2 1

5. When I must transfer a customer, I give the name, department, and phone number of the person receiving the call.   5 4 3 2 1

6. I give the caller my undivided attention.   5 4 3 2 1

7. I avoid side conversations of any kind during telephone conversations.   5 4 3 2 1

8. I don't interrupt the caller.   5 4 3 2 1

9. I slow my rate of speech slightly when explaining a complex matter or providing numbers.   5 4 3 2 1

10. I check with the caller to ensure understanding of transmitted information.   5 4 3 2 1

11. I thank the person for calling.   5 4 3 2 1

12. I allow the caller to hang up first.   5 4 3 2 1

Total: _____

Scoring:

50 or More   Excellent

41–49   Satisfactory

31–40   Needs improvement

30 or less   Unacceptable

Areas for Improvement

To the Facilitator After completion of the rating, form small groups to discuss the ratings, recommended actions for improvement, and the impact of ineffective phone skills on providing quality service. Conduct a large group discussion based on feedback from the subgroups and identify specific actions that can be taken for improvements on the job.

Behind the Scenes
Support Role Recognition

Leader

Recognition is a great form of positive reinforcement. However, those support staff who aren't on the front line can be forgotten when we hand out the award to the employees who had the highest sales or received the most customer accolades. Take time to single out those who are in support roles to help these outstanding service providers shine. And it isn't necessarily the actual award that counts as much as the spirit in which it is given.

ACTION

Create an award for those people who perform jobs that don't usually put them in the limelight. The recognition can take any form, but it should have a specific name and be given specifically to someone whose work is generally low profile or out of sight. You might want to call it the "Behind the Scenes Award" or the "Supporting Cast Award." Whatever you decide to call it, be certain to make a big deal about presenting the award and make sure that you present it on a regular basis.

Getting Down to Business
Customer Comment Cards

Individual

Comment cards are an important way of gathering information about the service or products you provide. However, when you ask your customers about how you are doing, also ask them about what you can do to meet their needs in the future. When you ask these questions, be sure to pose ones relevant to your specific customers. Consider what you want to learn from your customers, internal as well as external, and be prepared to do something about the feedback you receive.

● ●

ACTION

Create a comment card with three to five questions that would allow you to better understand the customer's perception of your service or products. The following are some examples:

1. If you could change one thing about the way we treat you, what would it be?

2. What one service or product could we provide to help meet your needs?

3. What could we do to make it easier for you to do business with us?

4. Would you recommend us to others? Why or why not?

5. Did you receive more than you expected? Why or why not?

6. If you were in charge of this organization, what one thing would you change and why?

7. How do we compare to other companies that provide similar products or services?

Hit the Heights
Customer Service Week

Leader

Celebrate Customer Service Week during the first full week in October and enjoy the benefits all year long! During this special week, you can take a big step toward boosting morale, motivation, and teamwork. Although recognition should be an ongoing process, this special event allows you to reward your frontline representatives and thank other departments for their support. By focusing on recognition in a big way, you will raise awareness of the important role that customer service plays and let your clients see your commitment to customer satisfaction. Whether your celebration lasts for one afternoon or an entire week, here are some ideas that can be incorporated into every celebration.

ACTIONS

- Create the right atmosphere by decorating with posters, a banner, and balloons.
- Host festive parties to show your appreciation for your hard-working representatives.
- Reward your representatives for their valuable contributions.

- Share information with everyone about how well the customer service unit performs.

- Acknowledge the role other departments play in meeting customer needs; use certificates of appreciation, service awards, and small gifts.

- Hone service skills by organizing skill-building training sessions.

- Show your appreciation for your customers with a thank-you message and a photograph of your service team.

- Host a stress-relief break and give your representatives suggestions and tools to reduce work pressures.

- Have fun with games, contests, and theme events to relieve stress and build teamwork.

- For more information on planning, materials, and sample agendas, check out www.csweek.com.

tip 82

Knowledge Is Power
Technical Training

Leader

We know that interpersonal skills alone do not make a good customer service experience. Service representatives need to know how to undertake the technical aspects of their jobs. Technical training empowers employees to perform the functional tasks that create results. These skills might involve such things as using the computer to access customer information, following correct processes and procedures, and being aware of the company's product line.

Careful attention to both technical *and* interpersonal skills training is important. Planning for customer service training must be a part of the overall strategy if you want to achieve excellence in your customer service efforts.

ACTIONS

- Review the competencies required to perform each job.

- List any gaps in the performance of each employee.

- Identify appropriate training and development strategies for each employee.

- Meet with each employee to prepare an individual development plan, with specific actions and deadlines.

- Follow up with employees at regular intervals to discuss progress, plan for application of new skills, and provide general feedback.

Concession Stand

Acknowledging Customer Concerns

Every customer service interaction involves two functions: maintaining the relationship with the customer and completing the task (transaction). If customers encounter some type of problem with the service transaction, they often are distressed about the situation. They react with a great deal of emotion. There are also times when the service provider needs to deliver bad news that will entail a negative reaction from the customer. When these situations occur, it is time for the employee to acknowledge the customer's feelings and reactions (relationship orientation) and then to progress toward resolution of the problem (task orientation). If you follow the guidelines for these two steps, you will move closer to maintaining a standard of exceptional customer service.

Step 1: Maintain the Relationship: Express Your Understanding

- Focus on recognizing the customer's point of view, and empathize.

- Be direct and forthright about the situation.

- Approach the situation with a positive attitude and tone.

- Do not place blame or make excuses.

Step 2: Maintain the Transaction: Specify What You Plan to Do

- Deal with the unique qualities of each situation.

- Explain why you are doing something.

- Explain how the customer will benefit from the solution.

- Give dates and deadlines.

- Make amends and try to find ways to "go the extra mile."

- Follow up and keep the customer informed of any progress.

Write On

Letters of Complaint

When a customer takes the time to send a letter of complaint about your company's product or service, it is critical to send an appropriate response. Most customers are probably upset when they write their letters, and if the response is not satisfactory, it will reinforce their negative feelings. These guidelines will help make your customer know that you—and the company—care about his or her feedback.

Respond promptly. The customer will be wondering if the complaint letter arrived and that the correct person received it. However, you might need a little time to resolve the issue before you can respond fully. Send the customer an initial response by note, phone, or fax and then follow up with a resolution letter within 2 weeks.

Do not use standardized letters. The content of such letters is too uniform and predictable to sound sincere. Each letter should be personalized to meet the customer's particular circumstances. This tells the customer that you understand the specific situation behind the complaint. Use a polite, understanding tone and never argue.

Thank the customer and apologize for any inconvenience. Let the customer know that you appreciate being made aware of the problem. Comment that this is an opportunity to improve service or correct a product failure, and explain in detail how you plan to make things right. Personally apologize for any trouble or inconvenience that the customer may have experienced.

Concentrate on the positive.   Focus on what you can do to alleviate the problem. This helps you move from a negative situation to one in which the customer will give your company another chance to meet future expectations.

Provide the appropriate amount of attention.   If you are addressing several different components of a problem, a single-page response may seem too abrupt and un-satisfying to a customer who has taken the time and effort to bring the problem to your attention. A personalized response letter of sufficient length will convey a sense of caring on behalf of your company.

Teamwork

Customer service is generally delivered by a group of people working together toward common goals. Service teamwork relies on the cooperation among individuals, departments, and organizations to provide effective customer service. Even when the service deliverer is a one-person enterprise, he or she relies on service partnerships with suppliers and associates to deliver effective customer service. Therefore, the highest level of service occurs when employees think of themselves, their colleagues, and their customers as one team, working together as part of the same process.

Because most organizations are made up of functional systems that interrelate, customer service can be viewed as the sum total of what an organization does to meet customer expectations and produce customer satisfaction. Although an individual may take a leading part in delivering customer service, it normally involves actions by a number of people in the company. To be successful in maintaining quality service for external customers, employees must be able to provide effective service to internal customers. Service teamwork therefore requires an interactive community of coworkers who collaborate, overcome, and achieve together.

By pooling resources and supporting one another, service teams can meet their goals and objectives faster and more easily. Working in teams allows the pooling of resources in order to meet the demands of an ever-expanding network of customers. This collaboration is especially important during the problem-solving process because the examination of diverse viewpoints can lead to new ways of viewing things, which bring about an expanded information base.

Partnering—that is, a win-win collaboration between two or more parties—increases productivity, fosters collaborative problem solving, and creates loyalty. Successful service partnerships engender trust in the people and organizations involved. Such trust leads to enhanced commitment to corporate goals, better customer service, higher morale and motivation, improved communication and information sharing, and better resolution of problems.

Teamwork and partnering are firmly rooted in issues of trust. This can have long-term implications for success or failure in relationships as well as the company's bottom line. When trust is low, organizations can decay and interactions deteriorate so that divisive politics, turf wars, and infighting might escalate. Finally, commitment to the organizational vision and strategy plummets, product and service quality deteriorates, morale declines, and customers leave. Therefore, the concerted effort of each individual team player must be fixed on building a trusting and trustworthy relationship with coworkers and clients alike.

Because teams are a logical approach to sharpening an organization's competitive edge, a blend of cooperation and competition naturally exists to help teams and organizations strive to do their best. A constructive competitive spirit can help motivate employees to maximize their contributions and work toward higher goals. As teams strive against competitors to perform at their highest levels, all group members combine efforts to experience a measure of success. Organizations are strongest when employees work together, delivering excellent value to clients. Team members capitalize on individual strengths while learning from one another.

Certain actions will help achieve a supportive team spirit, whether one is dealing with internal or external customers. These actions include respecting one another, sharing information, expressing needs, clarifying expectations, knowing the rules, relating outcomes, and developing relationships through trust, rapport, empathy, and understanding.

training 85

Candy Land
Group Decision Making

Goal   To facilitate effective decision making within a group. Participants will list candy items in order of the date of their creation.

Time Required   Approximately 40 to 50 minutes

Group Size   Subgroups of five or six persons each

Materials

● One copy of the Candy Land Worksheet and a pencil for each participant

● One copy of the Candy Land Answer Sheet for the facilitator

● Timer or clock

PROCESS

1. Introduce the session by telling the participants that there are thousands of different types of candy that are enjoyed by billions of people around the world. In the United States alone, the average person consumes about twenty-five pounds of candy each year. The participants will be members of companies vying for a position as marketing representative in the candy industry.

2. Form subgroups of five or six persons each.

3. Distribute one copy of the worksheet and a pencil to each participant. Read the directions at the top of the sheet.

4. Set the timer and allow exactly 20 minutes for completion of the task, giving a 2-minute warning before time expires. Call time.

5. Ask the subgroups to enter the appropriate rank numbers in the column marked Actual Ranking as you read aloud the answers found on the answer sheet. You may wish to include some of the background information provided or give only the rank number.

6. After all answers have been revealed, direct the participants to determine the value differences for each item by subtracting the smaller of the ranking numbers from the larger. When all values have been recorded in the final column, the total will be the sum of all the value differences.

7. Determine which subgroup had the *lowest* value difference total and announce that this group is awarded the marketing position.

8. Facilitate a large group discussion by asking the following questions:

   - How did you feel during this activity? Why?

   - What conditions in the group helped facilitate the decision-making process? What hindered it?

   - How well did group members use active listening skills? How was this evidenced?

   - Did all group members offer their ideas and opinions? If not, why not?

   - What guidelines can be instituted in a group setting to support effective decision making?

CANDY LAND WORKSHEET

Directions: Your group represents a company vying for a position as a marketing representative for the candy industry. To determine who will be the best company to hire, your future employer wants to see how much you know about the history of candy. Complete the Group Ranking column by placing the following candy items in order of their creation from the oldest (1) to the newest (15). You will have 20 minutes to complete the task, and then you will be given further instructions for scoring.

CANDY	GROUP RANKING	ACTUAL RANKING	DIFFERENCE
Baby Ruth			
5th Avenue			
Good & Plenty			
Hershey's Kisses			
Junior Mints			
Life Savers			
M&M's Plain Chocolate Candies			
Milk Duds			
Milky Way			
Necco Wafers			
Pez			
Snickers			
Starburst Fruit Chews			
3 Musketeers			
Tootsie Rolls			
TOTAL			

Note: Candy names are trademarks of the companies that produce them. All trademark rights are reserved to the trademark owners.

CANDY LAND ANSWER SHEET

1. **Good & Plenty (1893)**   Invented by Quaker Confectionery Co. in Philadelphia; oldest branded candy in the United States.

2. **Tootsie Rolls (1896)**   Invented by Leo Hirshfield of New York, who named them after his daughter.

3. **Necco Wafers (1901)**   Acronym for New England Confectionery Company; Admiral Byrd took 2½ tons of these pastel-colored candy disks to the South Pole in the 1930s because they don't melt.

4. **Hershey Kisses (1906)**   Invented by Milton S. Hershey of Lancaster, Pennsylvania; a popular theory is that the candy was named for the sound or motion of the chocolate being deposited during the manufacturing process.

5. **Life Savers (1912)**   Based on newly introduced life preservers; they originally came in peppermint flavor only.

6. **Baby Ruth (1920)**   Named after President Cleveland's daughter (not the famous ball player Babe Ruth).

7. **Milky Way (1923)**   Created to taste like a malted milk that would be available anywhere, any time.

8. **Milk Duds (1926)**   Milton Holloway's idea was to make perfectly round pieces, but found this was impossible, so he called them "duds."

9. **Pez (1927)**   Eduard Haas III originally marketed this candy as a compressed peppermint breath freshener for smokers; the name comes from the German word for peppermint: *pfefferminze.*

10. **Snickers (1930)**   Named for a favorite horse owned by the Mars family; it's currently the number one selling candy in the United States.

11. **3 Musketeers (1932)**   Originally made as three separate pieces of chocolate, vanilla, and strawberry nougat; rising costs and wartime restrictions required phasing out vanilla and strawberry.

12. **5th Avenue (1936)**   William Luden, of cough drop fame, made these for military use in World War II.

13. **M&M's Plain Chocolate Candies (1941)**   Introduced in response to slack chocolate sales in summer; inspired by Spanish Civil War soldiers eating pellets of chocolate in sugar coating.

14. **Junior Mints (1949)**   James Welch named these after his favorite Broadway stage play, *Junior Miss.*

15. **Starburst Fruit Chews (1960)**   Later fortified with 50 percent of the recommended daily allowance for vitamin C.

In and Out
Internal Customers

Goal   To identify the function of internal customer partnerships. Participants will create new internal support departments from assigned acronyms.

Time Required   Approximately 1 to 1½ hours

Group Size   Subgroups of three or four persons each, with a maximum of twenty-five participants

Materials

- One copy of the In and Out Worksheet and a pencil for each participant
- Three sheets of newsprint paper and a felt-tipped marker for each subgroup
- A flip chart and a felt-tipped marker for recording information
- Masking tape for posting newsprint sheets

● ●

PROCESS

1. Form subgroups of three or four persons each.

2. Distribute a copy of the worksheet and a pencil to each participant.

3. Referring to the directions, explain that each subgroup will select three of these well-known acronyms to identify departments that could be formed within the organization for the express purpose of assisting the participants in providing improved customer service. In addition, each group is to establish the objectives of these new units in terms of how the unit would assist or support them in meeting their service goals. The information will be listed on the sheet of newsprint paper provided. Groups will have 30 minutes in which to complete the work.

4. Distribute three sheets of newsprint paper and a felt-tipped marker to each subgroup.

5. Allow approximately 30 minutes, giving a 5-minute warning before time expires, and then stop group work.

6. Provide masking tape and have the groups post their sheets. Invite each subgroup in turn to report on the department name and list of objectives for each of the three acronyms chosen.

7. Explain that every employee in an organization is both a user and a provider of services. Improving internal customer service increases the likelihood of providing quality service and products to external customers.

8. Facilitate a discussion by asking the following questions:

    *   What role do you play in helping your internal customers perform their jobs?

    *   How does this help the organization as a whole provide better service to external customers?

    *   How can department liaisons support the improvement of the internal or external customer relationship?

    *   What specific actions can your team take to help your internal customers perform their jobs better?

IN AND OUT WORKSHEET

Directions: As a group, consider these well-known acronyms that might represent a new support "department" within your organization that assists you in providing improved customer service. Select three acronyms and identify the department that is represented by each set of letters. Next, establish the objectives of each new unit in terms of how it could assist or support you in meeting your team's service goals.

ASAP	FYI	LCD	RSVP
CIA	GED	MBA	SWAT
CPR	HMO	NFL	VCR

Acronym 1:

Department Name:

Objectives:

Acronym 2:

Department Name:

Objectives:

Acronym 3:

Department Name:

Objectives:

Mind the Details

Individual vs. Team Performance

Goal To examine how teamwork influences performance. Participants will answer questions relating to visual aspects of common items, first as individuals and then as a team.

Time Required
Approximately 30 to 40 minutes

Group Size
Subgroups of five or six persons each

Materials

- One copy of the Mind the Details Worksheet and a pencil for each participant

- Clock or timer

● ●

PROCESS

1. Form subgroups of five or six persons each.

2. Distribute one copy of the worksheet and a pencil to each participant.

3. Tell the participants that each person will have 5 minutes to answer the ten questions alone. Answers are to be recorded in the Individual Response column.

4. Signal for the participants to begin, time for 5 minutes, and then stop the activity.

5. Explain that members of each group now will have 15 minutes to decide on a group answer for each question. These answers will be recorded in the Group Response column.

6. Signal for the groups to begin discussion and time for 5 minutes, giving a 1-minute warning before time expires. Stop the activity.

7. Direct the participants to check the responses recorded in each column against the answers you will be presenting. They are to place an X in front of each wrong response.

8. Reveal the following answers to the questions: (1) Benjamin Franklin, (2) right, (3) bottom, (4) five, (5) Colombia, (6) Nebraska, (7) blue, (8) "Liberty," (9) TUV, (10) Sirius (Dog Star).

9. Ask the participants to count the number of correct answers for each column and place the appropriate scores on the worksheet.

10. Facilitate a large group discussion by asking the following questions:

    • What aspects of this activity made it difficult?

    • Did you perform better individually or as a group? Why?

    • How accurate were your group's answers overall? What factors influenced this outcome?

    • What could your group have done to improve its performance?

    • Why is teamwork important when providing service to your customers?

    • In what specific ways does your work team pull together in your organization?

    • What are some additional things your team could do to become more effective?

MIND THE DETAILS WORKSHEET

Question	Individual Response	Group Response
1. Whose face appears on the U.S. $100 bill?		
2. In which hand does the Statue of Liberty hold the torch?		
3. On traffic lights, in which position is green located?		
4. When considering dice, which number appears on the side directly opposite the two?		
5. On a map of South America, what country borders Venezuela on the west?		
6. On a map of the United States, what state lies directly north of Kansas?		
7. What is the background color of the United Nations flag?		
8. Besides "In God We Trust," what single word appears on the front of every United States coin?		
9. What letter sequence corresponds to the number 8 on a telephone?		
10. What is the brightest star in the night sky?		
Scores		

On Course

Communication, Reliability, and Trust

Goal   To explore the impact of team communication, reliability, and trust on customer expectations. Participants will be blindfolded and will traverse an obstacle course at the verbal direction of two guides.

Time Required
Approximately 40 to 50 minutes

Group Size
Eight to twelve participants

Note   This activity is best conducted with an intact work group. Because of safety issues, be sure to consider your audience in terms of age, physical limitations, and so forth before attempting this exercise.

Materials

- One long rope (approximately 6 feet)
- One blindfold for each participant, less two
- A map of the obstacle course

• •

PROCESS

1. Prior to the session, prepare a large indoor space with an obstacle course. Place chairs, desks, cardboard boxes, and other objects around the room in a fairly challenging configuration so that participants need to go around, under, or over objects. Be careful to address all safety concerns before proceeding with this activity. Draw a map showing the obstacles and the course that the participants are to navigate.

2. Ask the group to select two participants to act as guides during the activity. Explain that the job of the guides is to get the entire group through the obstacle course.

3. Explain that anyone who wishes to opt out as a blindfolded player can observe the group actions silently from the sidelines. Distribute a blindfold to the remaining players and ask them to place the blindfolds over their eyes so that they cannot see. Give the rope to the blindfolded participants and direct them to hold on to it throughout the activity. *Note:* Emphasize the importance of going slowly during the exercise.

4. Provide the guides with the map showing the course through which the participants are to navigate. Explain that the guides are to give verbal instructions only. *Note:* If someone feels unsafe at any time, stop the activity immediately and address the safety issues.

5. Signal to start the activity. Make observations of the progress that the team makes and the instructions being provided by the guides. Stop the activity when the group completes the course or after approximately 15 minutes if the task has not been completed.

6. Facilitate a large group discussion by asking the following questions:

- What process was used to select the two guides? What factors influenced the choice?

- What specifically did the guides do that helped you get through the course? Did they do anything that hindered you? If so, what?

- Did those blindfolded rely solely on communication from the guides? If not, what other sources did you rely on to traverse the course? What did you do to help one another through the course?

- How did the size of the group affect performance? Why?

- What kind of communication did you need to perform this exercise well? How did the communication process affect your expectations of the performance of the guides?

- Did you feel that you could trust the actions of your guides and the people around you? What factors influenced your impressions of reliability and trust?

- In the workplace, how effectively does your team work together in terms of trust and reliability? What factors influence this?

- Did the guides meet or exceed your expectations of their performance? What factors influenced your impressions? How does this relate to meeting your customers' expectations?

- What specific actions can be taken on the job to improve the team's ability to work together to meet customer expectations?

Open Account
Team Environment

Goal   To explore ways to improve conditions within the current team environment. Participants will use pictures to develop a verbal account of an ideal service team environment.

Time Required
Approximately 1 hour

Group Size
Subgroups of three or four persons each from an intact service team

Materials

- One Open Account Picture Cards set of eight cards for each subgroup

- One newsprint sheet and glue stick for each subgroup

- One sheet of blank paper and a pencil for each participant

- One magazine containing a variety of pictures for each subgroup

- One pair of scissors for each subgroup

- Four 3" × 5" index cards and a felt-tipped pen for each subgroup

- Masking tape for posting newsprint sheets

- Flip chart and felt-tipped marker for facilitator

● ●

PROCESS

1. Prior to the session, prepare one picture card set for each subgroup by cutting each sheet into four individual pictures.

2. At the session, form subgroups of three or four persons each.

3. Distribute one set of the following items to each subgroup: picture card set, magazine, scissors, four index cards, felt-tipped pen, newsprint sheet, and glue stick. Provide one sheet of blank paper and a pencil to each participant.

4. Explain that each subgroup will have 30 minutes to develop a visual and verbal account of an ideal service team environment. This will be done by using all eight picture cards provided and adding any four pictures obtained either by cutting them from the magazine or drawing them on the index cards. Use the glue stick to paste all twelve pictures onto the newsprint sheet, creating a visual representation to guide the group's narrative that will be presented to the whole group (the blank paper may be used for taking notes).

5. Allow approximately 30 minutes to complete the assigned task, giving a 5-minute warning before time expires.

6. Provide masking tape and direct the groups to post their sheets.

7. Ask a member of each group in turn to relate the narrative of an ideal team environment as he or she references the appropriate pictures on the newsprint sheet.

8. Facilitate a large group discussion by asking the following questions, recording responses as noted:

   • What were the similarities among the various accounts?

   • What were the differences?

- How difficult was it to use the pictures to develop your account? Why?

- What role did perception play in this activity?

- How can certain expectations for an ideal team environment affect employee motivation?

- Do such expectations have an impact on service delivery? If so, how?

- What specific actions can the team take to alter current conditions that might help in moving toward this ideal picture? (Record on the flip chart.)

OPEN ACCOUNT PICTURE CARDS 1

OPEN ACCOUNT PICTURE CARDS 2

Port of Call
Partnering Strategies

Goal   To facilitate group interaction for sharing best practices for partnering. Participants will assemble into groups based on various parts of a ship and similar destinations and then share strategies for partnering with customers and support units.

Time Required   Approximately 40 to 50 minutes

Group Size   Subgroups of six or seven persons each

Note   This exercise works best with a large group of participants.

Materials

- One index card for each participant
- One card-stock sheet for each group
- Flip chart and felt-tipped marker for facilitator

PROCESS

1. Prior to the session, prepare the materials as follows. A table tent for each group can be made by folding a card-stock sheet in half and writing the name of a different port of call (for example, Buenos Aires, Naples, New York, Marseilles, Singapore, Stockholm) on each. You also will need a set of seven index cards for each port of call being used, with each card in the set containing the name of the port plus one of the following parts of a ship: Hull, Deck, Anchor, Rudder, Stern, Bow, and Mast. You will have seven cards for each port, and you will select enough ports to accommodate one card for each participant. *Note:* Some groups may have fewer than seven members, depending on the total number of participants. Adjust the card sets accordingly so that there are at least six ship parts used per designated port.

2. At the beginning of the session, randomly distribute one card to each participant.

3. Explain that participants are to locate a complete set of ship parts that are going to the same port of call as listed on their cards. Once the entire ship has been assembled, the group is to meet at the appropriate table where its destination is indicated.

4. After all the groups have assembled, ask team members to introduce themselves and tell their functional role in the organization.

5. After several minutes, tell the groups that they will spend approximately 20 minutes sharing personal strategies, tips, and techniques for partnering with external customers as well as internal work units. Explain that partnering is a win-win collaboration between two or more entities committed to a mutual goal.

6. Allow approximately 20 minutes and then stop the discussion.

7. Facilitate a large group discussion by asking the following questions:

    - Why were various parts of a ship but similar destinations used to get you into groups? *(For example, there is diversity within teams, but all members work toward a common goal.)*

    - How does your answer to the previous question apply to teamwork?

    - Why is it important to rely on partnering with others when providing customer service?

    - What are some examples of the strategies for partnering with customers and work units in the organization that can help you perform your job more effectively? (List the ideas on a flip chart.)

Seeing STARS
Group Interdependence

Goal
To explore the concept of "co-opetition" (a blend of cooperation and competition) through group interdependence. Participants will unscramble words by finding common missing letter sets.

Time Required
Approximately 40 to 50 minutes

Group Size
Ten to thirty individuals

Materials

- One Seeing STARS Card for each participant
- One Seeing STARS Card Sets Answer Sheet for each subgroup
- One sheet of paper and a pencil for each participant
- Small box or large envelope as receptacle for cards
- Timer or stopwatch

● Flip chart and felt-tipped marker for recording

● Prize for the winning group

● ●

PROCESS

1. Prior to the session, prepare the five card sets by duplicating each sheet onto card stock and cutting each sheet into individual cards. (Alternatively, print the letters and identification symbol for each card onto a 3" × 5" index card.) Allow a card for each participant with at least one card from each of the five different symbol sets, and place these into a small box or large envelope, mixing them thoroughly. Position a flip chart and felt-tipped marker in a centrally located area of the room.

2. At the session, explain that the participants will be practicing their problem-solving abilities, first as individuals and then as groups. *Do not reveal the name of the activity at this point.*

3. Distribute one card to each participant by randomly drawing it from the receptacle. Provide each participant with one sheet of paper and a pencil.

4. Say to the participants, "Upon my signal, each person is to work alone to unscramble the letters on the card provided, determining the one missing letter indicated by a question mark that will complete the word. You will have one minute to complete the task."

5. Signal for work to begin. Allow exactly 1 minute for completion of the task, and then call time.

6. Tell the participants that a single word can be formed by combining the missing letters from all representative sets. These groups will be formed by locating four other individuals who have cards with varying symbols in the lower left corner. The first group to write the correct word on the flip chart is the winner and will be awarded a prize. However, only *one* group can become the winner.

7. Signal for the activity to begin, then stop when one group writes the word "STARS" on the flip chart. Assign a prize to the winning group.

8. Distribute a copy of the Seeing STARS Card Sets Answer Sheet to each group. Ask the group members to review the unscrambled words for their own subgroup's card set.

9. Allow a few minutes for group discussion and then ask the following questions:

   - How did you feel while performing the activity?

   - What problem-solving approach did you use to unscramble your initial word? Was it effective? Why?

   - At what point did you discover that all the words within a symbol set shared a *common* missing letter? How did this information become known? How did it affect the overall task?

   - How well did participants interact with one another while trying to determine the final word? How much did the goal of "winning" affect this?

   - What role did cooperation play in this activity? What role did competition play?

10. Tell the participants that there is a term, *co-opetition,* that embodies both coopera-tion and competition. It is the blend of both of these concepts that works to help teams strive to their best. Generating a constructive competitive spirit that moti-vates group members to maximize their contributions enables organizations to achieve goals more effectively. However, this competitive spirit must be combined with an effort to cooperate with other groups.

11. Facilitate a large group discussion by asking the following questions:

   - How does the concept of co-opetition apply in this activity?

   - In what specific ways can employees work together to become service "STARS"? *(Refer to word on flip chart.)*

   - How can we relate this activity to service situations in the workplace?

Source: Adapted from Ukens, L. L. (2004). Get smart: A co-opetition activity. In *The 2004 Pfeiffer annual (Training)* (pp. 69–78). San Fran-cisco: Pfeiffer.

SEEING STARS CARD SET 1

NDI
GLI?

★ 1

TNE
RAO?

★ 4

YAIE
DMD?

★ 2

MER
UED?

★ 5

CEE
MH?

★ 3

RTA
ER?

★ 6

SEEING STARS CARD SET 2

ERA
SNE?

► 1

GRI
NS?

► 2

EFR
DID?

► 3

PSE
LA?

► 4

ATR
NSI?

► 5

SIEN
CDA?

► 6

SEEING STARS CARD SET 3

GEA
RG?

● 1

TDE
FE?

● 4

ECP
SE?

● 2

BUE
ESC?

● 5

EIL
MTC?

● 3

TSNI
ROS?

● 6

SEEING STARS CARD SET 4

TFO
OG?

■ 1

SAC
PEL?

■ 4

UDO
GEP?

■ 2

TIA
TS?

■ 5

EAE
WHT?

■ 3

IETC
LCE?

■ 6

SEEING STARS CARD SET 5

TLA RPE? ◆ 1	PLM DAE? ◆ 4
EAD RE? ◆ 2	CMU ONE? ◆ 5
NIR IA? ◆ 3	LPER AUE? ◆ 6

SEEING STARS CARD SETS ANSWER SHEET

SET 1 – "S"

★ 1 *S*LIDING

★ 2 DI*S*MAYED

★ 3 *S*CHEME

★ 4 TREA*S*ON

★ 5 RE*S*UMED

★ 6 ARRE*S*T

SET 2 – "T"

▶ 1 EARNES*T*

▶ 2 S*T*RING

▶ 3 DRIF*T*ED

▶ 4 S*T*APLE

▶ 5 *T*RANSIT

▶ 6 DIS*T*ANCE

SET 3 – "A"

● 1 G*A*RAGE

● 2 ES*C*APE

● 3 CLIM*A*TE

● 4 DEFE*A*T

● 5 BEC*A*USE

● 6 *A*RSONIST

SET 4 – "R"

- ◼ 1   FO*R*GOT
- ◼ 2   G*R*OUPED
- ◼ 3   WEATHE*R*
- ◼ 4   PA*R*CELS
- ◼ 5   A*R*TIST
- ◼ 6   ELECT*R*IC

SET 5 – "S"

- ◆ 1   PLA*S*TER
- ◆ 2   ERA*S*ED
- ◆ 3   RAI*S*IN
- ◆ 4   *S*AMPLED
- ◆ 5   CON*S*UME
- ◆ 6   PLEA*S*URE

To the Letter

Time-Constrained Team Performance

Goal   To work on a task as a team under the pressure of time constraints. In a collective group effort, participants will list the names of cities beginning with the letters from A to Z.

Time Required   Approximately 20 to 30 minutes

Group Size   Subgroups of four to six persons each

Materials

- One copy of the To the Letter Worksheet and a pencil for each subgroup

- Timer or stopwatch

PROCESS

1. Form subgroups of four to six persons each. Ask the members of each subgroup to count off for their order of play during the activity.

2. Distribute one copy of the worksheet and a pencil to player 1 in each subgroup.

3. Explain that the goal is to list the names of as many cities as possible on the worksheet, one by one in alphabetical order, moving vertically, one column at a time. Play passes from one group member to the next, as in a relay race. All the answers in Column 1 must be attempted before Column 2 can be started. For example, Player 1 writes *Akron* for the letter A in Column 1, then passes the worksheet and pencil to Player 2, who fills in *Baltimore* for B, and so on. Other members of the group may *not* make suggestions if a player cannot think of an answer during his or her turn. A player may choose to skip a letter by placing an X in the appropriate block. Duplicate answers are *not* allowed. Groups will have 5 minutes to complete the task.

4. Time the activity for exactly 5 minutes, giving a 1-minute warning before time expires, and then stop the groups.

5. Direct the subgroups to tally the total number of words entered on the worksheet. The group with the greatest number of words is declared the winner.

6. Facilitate a large group discussion by asking the following questions:

   - In what ways did the time pressure affect your group's productivity?

   - How did individuals feel if they were unable to find an answer for a particular letter? Why?

   - How supportive were other members of your group? How was this evidenced?

   - What impact, if any, did skipping letters have on the overall performance of the groups? What factors might account for this?

   - Would your play have changed any if you had been able to go back to fill in missing answers? Why or why not?

   - What relationship does this activity have to providing service to internal and external customers in general? Specifically, to following work processes and procedures? To relying on collaborative work actions?

TO THE LETTER WORKSHEET

	COLUMN 1	COLUMN 2	COLUMN 3
A			
B			
C			
D			
E			
F			
G			
H			
I			
J			
K			
L			
M			
N			
O			
P			
Q			
R			
S			
T			
U			
V			
W			
X			
Y			
Z			

A Matter of Trust

Team Member Trust

A team's ability to function effectively is affected by the amount of individual trust that group members share. Trust affects the confidence that group members have in the integrity, ability, character, and truth of other individuals in the team. Assessing oneself in various aspects of trust-related issues is a critical step in identifying areas for improvement.

Directions: Respond to each of the following statements as if the other members of your service team were evaluating you as a group member. Rate yourself according to the scale below and then identify your perceived areas for improvement.

5 = Always   4 = Usually   3 = Sometimes   2 = Rarely   1 = Never

1.	I share as much information as possible with the team.	5 4 3 2 1
2.	I avoid taking credit for other people's ideas and work.	5 4 3 2 1
3.	I follow through on promises that I make to others.	5 4 3 2 1
4.	I willingly admit my own mistakes.	5 4 3 2 1
5.	I avoid placing blame on others and focus only on the issues.	5 4 3 2 1
6.	I keep the confidences of others.	5 4 3 2 1
7.	I demonstrate respect for the opinions of others.	5 4 3 2 1
8.	I honestly and openly express my opinions.	5 4 3 2 1
9.	I actively seek out the opinions of others.	5 4 3 2 1
10.	I directly confront issues with people rather than avoid them.	5 4 3 2 1
11.	I treat other team members with honesty and fairness.	5 4 3 2 1
12.	I am consistent in my words and actions.	5 4 3 2 1

Total: _____

Scoring:

55 or more	Excellent trust level
45–54	High trust level
35–44	Low trust level
34 or less	Needs work!

Targeted Areas for Improvement:

_____   _____

_____   _____

To the Facilitator   Distribute a copy of the assessment to each team member in printed form or by e-mail. Collect the completed evaluations and calculate the average scores for each statement. Conduct a follow-up discussion session to report the results. For each item, ask team members if they agree or disagree with the general assessment reported. Determine those areas in which there is general disagreement and ask for specific examples. Identify aspects of the work environment that might contribute to lower levels of trust among team members and list specific actions that the group as a whole can take to improve trust within the team.

Team Checkup
Group Effectiveness

Quality customer service requires strong leadership; skilled management; effective team-work; and skilled, caring, and motivated people on the front line. This partnering spirit also must be supported by appropriate knowledge, skills, processes, and standards.

Directions: Assume the average situation when responding to the following statements.

1. When handling telephone calls from customers, all team members use a uniform established greeting.

   Strongly Disagree   1   2   3   4   5   Strongly Agree

2. Team members have been given comprehensive training on the techniques needed to handle and resolve customer complaints.

   Strongly Disagree   1   2   3   4   5   Strongly Agree

3. New employees are well educated on such issues as dress code, office regulations, and work environment.

   Strongly Disagree   1   2   3   4   5   Strongly Agree

4. Team members are skilled at knowing how and when to use a variety of questioning techniques in their customer interactions.

   Strongly Disagree   1   2   3   4   5   Strongly Agree

5. Team members know how to present negative information to customers using a positive approach.

   Strongly Disagree   1   2   3   4   5   Strongly Agree

6. Team members do a great job of building rapport with customers and making them feel good about doing business with us.

   Strongly Disagree   1   2   3   4   5   Strongly Agree

7. Customers are usually impressed by the high level of care our team provides to them.

   Strongly Disagree   1   2   3   4   5   Strongly Agree

8. When a team member is having a bad day, negative emotions are never obvious to a customer.

   Strongly Disagree   1   2   3   4   5   Strongly Agree

9. When an individual team member has performance problems, the leader uses an effective coaching process to help.

   Strongly Disagree   1   2   3   4   5   Strongly Agree

10. In our team, coworkers are treated as well as we try to treat our customers.

    Strongly Disagree   1   2   3   4   5   Strongly Agree

To the Facilitator   Distribute a copy of the assessment to each team member in printed form or by e-mail. Collect the completed evaluations and calculate the average scores for each statement. Conduct a follow-up discussion session to report the results and to explore issues that may be affecting team performance. Identify specific actions that the team can take to improve its ability to provide quality-driven customer service. You can use the survey to monitor improvement efforts by redistributing the evaluation form in approximately 3 to 6 months and comparing ratings.

Bank on It

Peer Recognition

Leader

Create a "Days Off Bank" and use it to reward and motivate employees by allowing team members to recognize their peers who work hard. This system will build a sense of cooperation within the team because it puts recognition into the hands of coworkers. By limiting the number of days in the bank available during a set period of time, you encourage individuals to present the awards only when they are warranted.

> Note   Be sure to check with your Human Resources department to verify that this procedure complies with company policy.

· ·

ACTION

Create a "Days Off Bank":

1. Depending on the size of your team, create a bank of days (approximately ten to twenty-five) that will cover a one-year period.

2. Create a poster board representing the bank and place the number of days in the account. Print the names of each team member in columnar form along the side of the poster.

3. Obtain a supply of small self-stick labels that will be used to signify one "dollar" each and place them in an envelope attached to the poster.

4. Explain to team members that they can recognize the accomplishments of their colleagues by assigning them one dollar each time they feel that the colleague has performed work "above and beyond the call of duty." The person who is assigning the award is to write a brief description of the work performed on one of the labels and place it on the poster next to the name of the person.

5. When an employee earns ten dollars, he or she can cash them in for one of the days in the bank.

6. As days are used, check off the labels cashed in and reduce the number of days available in the bank.

Get on Board

Peer Feedback

Leader

Team members may be reluctant to compliment one another, but peer encouragement is a powerful motivator. To facilitate a healthy exchange of feedback, you can use a Feedback Train to provide a fun outlet for everyone to leave some positive words for fellow workers. This not only motivates the group but also provides some new ideas for ways to meet business objectives.

ACTION

Create a Feedback Train for team members:

1. On a flip-chart sheet or poster board, create a large image of a train, similar to the one shown in the illustration. Be sure to include enough cars to accommodate all team members.

2. Title the engine with your name as leader and place the name of each team member under a train car.

3. Post the sheet or board in a prominent location in the work area.

4. Provide each team member with a packet of self-stick notes or place them at the top of the posted sheet or board.

5. Encourage team members to write positive remarks about how others in the group have contributed to the team's efforts. The notes should be posted on the appropriate train car of the team member.

6. *Optional:* Hold a recognition ceremony for the team member with the most positive comments in a given time period.

Rely on Me
Team Trust

Individual

Trust and sincerity are fundamental to the success of any team and to building a successful relationship with your customers. Communication, consistency, and cooperative initiatives are critical aspects of maintaining trust. Remember—being trustworthy earns trust.

ACTIONS

- *Be cooperative.* Use the Golden Rule and treat others as you would like to be treated.

- *Listen attentively.* Pay careful attention to what group members say and give them good verbal and nonverbal feedback.

- *Ask questions and verify understanding.* Discuss ideas and opinions to help solve problems and avoid conflict resulting from misconceptions.

- *Consider personal feelings.* Understand the opinions of others and deal with emotions to better accept ideas and behaviors.

- *Communicate openly.* Talk about things candidly and accept what others have to say.

- *Be neutral.* Keep an open mind and don't make hasty judgments.

- *Be reliable.* Do what you say you will and never break a confidence.

- *Support teamwork.* Encourage one another to work toward personal and professional growth.

- *Accept accountability.* Honestly admit when you are wrong and learn from your mistakes.

- *Don't get defensive.* Do not attack others or place blame in an effort to protect your self-esteem.

Rivalry or Revelry
Constructive Competition

Leader

Teams often suffer from complacency because they have been shielded from competition. Competition should not be confused with controversy or conflict, however. A blend of both cooperation and competition is necessary to help teams strive to do their best. Generating a constructive competitive spirit that motivates employees to maximize their contributions enables an organization to achieve its goals.

● ●

ACTION

Hold a "naming" contest:

1. Generate an environment of friendly competition by running a contest whereby service teams or departments can enter a suggested name for a new product or service.

2. When all the entries have been received, send out the suggestions and ask employees to vote on the top three names.

3. Be sure to reward the winners with group awards, such as a luncheon or a team trophy, so that you emphasize the cooperative aspect of the team effort.

Team Talent

Resource Directory

Leader

Teamwork is an important aspect of providing excellent customer service because we often need to rely on others to provide information and problem-solving assistance. By identifying the resources available within your team, you take the first step in creating a strong support network.

ACTION

Create a team talent directory:

1. Devise a questionnaire for the team that helps individuals identify their uniqueness and capabilities.

2. List the names of all the team members along with their talents, skills, and interests.

3. Keep the book current and add new skills as they develop.

4. Keep the directory in a prominent location for easy access and consider making copies for distribution to other departments.

5. Team members should be urged to use the "experts" in the directory to help gather information and solve problems.

Confront with Care

Team Conflict Management

When team members or support units within the organization work together, disagreements can occur in terms of coworkers' behavior, attitude, or opinions. There are times when these situations can cause a breakdown in group performance or result in division within the team itself. From time to time, you may need to confront these issues directly to keep things running smoothly on the job. The next time you are faced with a personal confrontation with a teammate, try using the following method to smooth out conflicts and solve problems when working with others on an ongoing basis.

1. State the problem.   The key to effective confrontation is to focus on the problem behavior or issue and not on the person. When you talk to the other person, do it one-on-one and in private. Remain calm and do not make accusations. Try to keep anger, blame, and annoyance out of the tone of your voice and use clear, unemotional words.

2. Listen and restate.   After stating the problem, sit back and wait. By taking a moment to pause, you let the other person feel free to respond. Carefully listen to what is being said and don't make assumptions about what will be said. After the other person has finished speaking, acknowledge his or her feelings and clarify the message by restating the information that he or she presented.

3. If necessary, address the problem behavior or issue again.   If the person provides a good explanation for the behavior (for example, he or she was unable to obtain information), you can immediately move on to the final step of problem solving. However, you may need once again to confront the issue from your perspective. It is important to frame your opinions in terms of solving the problem, especially in terms of facilitating group performance, and this may necessitate taking on some of the responsibility for why the problem behavior or issue occurred in the first place. This approach indicates a willingness to share the problem with the other party.

   Should you feel that you are unable to move into a state of problem solving at this point, repeat the middle steps again and again until the other person is ready to move on. This process may appear to be time-consuming, but it is a worthwhile effort because it can effectively eliminate the potential for strong emotions that could cloud the issues.

4. Begin to find solutions.   The final step is to restate the initial problem to make sure you both agree on the issues involved and then to identify and discuss a variety of alternatives. In order to commit to a resolution of the problem, encourage the other person to select one or two action steps that directly help resolve the issue. Offer assistance or help the other person find appropriate resources. It is important to emphasize the benefits to the team of resolving the problem.

5. Follow up.   Monitor the situation in terms of the original problem or issue to see if things have been resolved. If there is improvement, provide positive feedback to the other person. If not, use this technique to start the process of confrontation again.

Opposition Position
Constructive Competition

The use of teams has emerged as a logical approach to sharpening an organization's competitive edge. Although the need for cooperation among team members is readily promoted, the concept of working as a cohesive unit also implies some underlying competition, because team members unite so that their efforts yield better results than those of any other team. Tapping into the motivational energy of constructive competition can help team members meet common goals. Healthy competition creates a positive buzz around achieving top performance. This type of competition encourages team members to use their creativity to meet goals, and to feel pride in their own performance. When people compete as a team against other teams, they fulfill many psychological needs. Teamwork creates a positive internal environment that results in improved customer service and stronger client partnerships. The information provided here can guide the group leader or manager in developing processes and procedures that enhance teamwork.

Social Needs

Competition motivates members of a work group to cooperate and work together as a team because they identify with the team.

1. Team members need to be physically located so as to encourage interaction with one another.

2. Team sports and after-work social events sponsored by the company provide additional opportunities for interaction.

3. Team apparel supports identification with the group.

Security Needs

Competition can be related to the necessity of at least meeting the achievements of other teams in competitive companies. Doing so is generally accepted as a requirement for remaining employed and allows for growth and development of both the organization and its members.

1. Individual and team performance must be measured through regular evaluations.

2. Team members need to know the strengths and talents of all individuals on the team.

3. Team members should receive training and development opportunities.

Self-Esteem Needs

Competition instills an aura of importance to all tasks, no matter how dull or uninteresting they may seem to be. Because of this, the ego of the individual employee becomes attached to the results achieved by the team.

1. Team assignments are designed so that members provide task support for one another.

2. Team guidelines are established in regard to honest and ethical behavior.

3. Team members share insights into individual expectations, behaviors, and values.

Achievement Needs

As members of a team, individuals gain the opportunity to receive the special recognition and attention associated with being the winner in a competitive situation.

1. Team members are involved in setting common goals.

2. Team members are encouraged to provide mutual feedback on task performance.

3. Team rewards should be given to recognize the efforts of all members of the team.

Appendix A
Internal Customer Service

Customer satisfaction needs to become a strategic priority for organizations, defined as a performance expectation to which every employee must be held accountable. Expectations regarding internal customers are at the same high level as those for external customers, so it is important to cultivate strong working relationships among all company functions. Individuals and teams often rely on the services of other employees and work units in order to satisfy external customers, but they also function as service suppliers to internal customers somewhere along the line. This interdependence requires employees to develop constructive approaches for sharing resources and working with other organizational units to meet service objectives.

Internal customers expect colleagues to be responsive to long-term needs and to have services available that allow them to meet their objectives. In the short term, they expect others to respond quickly and effectively to unforeseen needs. Further, whatever services they receive, internal customers anticipate receiving them in the same manner every time. Standards for performance and internal quality must be established to increase accountability.

Adequate resources are necessary to meet internal commitments, and an important part of providing them is the understanding of how other departments function within the organization. Feedback is another essential component for problem resolution and continuous improvement efforts. Internal customers need to be kept informed on the progress of all work, especially involving delays and problems. Problem-solving sessions and the review of policies and procedures will help ensure continuous improvement.

Just as in their interactions with external customers, employees must display a high level of professionalism when dealing with internal customers. High-quality interactions can smooth over disappointment and frustration when expectations can't be met; they build trust and credibility for long-term working relationships. Recognizing the superior efforts of internal service suppliers helps forge a stronger team spirit for meeting organizational goals. Developing a culture of collaboration can make this happen. Partnering fosters shared problem solving, reenergizes work units, and creates loyalty.

Here are some interventions that are particularly recommended for **internal customer service:**

Awareness

10   On the Line: Credibility

Communication

18   From Me to You: Focus on Others

32   Return Policy: Feedback Guidelines

Planning

34   Color Quest: Limited Resources

36   Flow Motion: Work Process Improvement

50   Setting the Bar: Service Standards

Problem Solving

57   Nominally Speaking: Nominal Group Technique

63   Feelings Check-In: Conflict Reaction Assessment

64   Share to Be Aware: Interdepartmental Problem Solving

Quality

79   Behind the Scenes: Support Role Recognition

81   Hit the Heights: Customer Service Week

Teamwork

86 In and Out: Internal Customers

90 Port of Call: Partnering Strategies

91 Seeing STARS: Group Interdependence

97 Rely on Me: Team Trust

98 Rivalry or Revelry: Constructive Competition

100 Confront with Care: Team Conflict Management

101 Opposition Position: Constructive Competition

Appendix B
Call Centers

The telephone call center can be one of a company's most important functions. The employees that staff the call center are often the first line of contact with current and potential customers. In essence, they *are* the company. To manage the rising level of customer expectations, these service providers need both skills and knowledge, as well as an environment that cultivates their ability to use them.

The work involves being up-to-date not only on product knowledge and company policy but also on ever-changing technology, which includes phone and computer systems. There is constant activity, and customer interactions are often monitored. When you top all this off with round-the-clock coverage, call centers can be a pressure cooker for stress and low employee morale. To avoid employee burnout, managers must incorporate stress reduction interventions and motivational challenges into the environment.

Because a main feature of most call centers is problem solving, service providers often deal with customers who are upset, angry, or confused; the ability to create solutions must be combined with empathy and understanding. When face-to-face interaction is eliminated, verbal communication becomes a critical factor. To be effective, it must be clear, concise, and correct. Active listening, probing, and paraphrasing skills keep the two-way communication process flowing. Voice quality and tone combine with telephone etiquette skills to provide the foundation for high customer satisfaction.

Because it is critical that the service representative be both efficient and accurate, managers must set appropriate goals and performance standards. In addition, such planning strategies as work organization, time management, and resource utilization help lay an appropriate foundation for meeting customer needs for information and problem solving.

Here are some interventions that are particularly recommended for **call center** staff:

Awareness

8   Stressing the Positive: Workplace Stressors

13 Keep It Cool: Job Pressure

14 Stress Buster: Stress Reduction

15 Meltdown: Dealing with Anger

Communication

17 Blueprints for Success: Verbal Instructions

19 Negative Ten-dency: Word Usage

21 Say What You Mean: Concise Verbal Information

23 Summary Judgment: Listening

28 Sound Advice: Voice Quality

29 Crossing the Border: International Communication

31 Attention, Please: Keeping the Customer's Attention

Planning

42 Desk Stress: Organization

50 Setting the Bar: Service Standards

51 Tackling Time Wasters: Time Management

Problem Solving

52 Comic Relief: Analyzing Problem Situations

53 Dialing Dilemma: Telephone Logic Problem

Quality

78 May I Help You? Telephone Etiquette

83 Concession Stand: Acknowledging Customer Concerns

Appendix C
Retail

Retail functions can include equal amounts of both sales and problem solving. The main ingredient, however, is the actual face-to-face interaction with the customer. Customers will not be impressed by a fake smile and "canned" or impersonal words. An inauthentic and robotic "Thank you, please come back" won't do the trick. What really counts for customers is a quick response, personalized attention, positive behavior, and helpfulness.

How well a service provider communicates with the customer can make or break a transaction. Approximately half of what we communicate comes across through visual clues, such as facial expressions, body movement, and posture. This "body language" is a very powerful component of personal interactions. Retail employees need both verbal and nonverbal communication skills to manage the company-customer relationship that keeps people coming back as loyal customers.

In terms of making sales, the manner of persuasion and the degree to which service providers assert themselves can influence the outcome. Being aware of the uniqueness of individual customers helps employees avoid making assumptions. At the same time, what a customer thinks he or she needs isn't always correct. Appropriate probing skills can help the customer make the most appropriate choices from among a variety of alternatives. This extra attention to customer needs relies on the service representative's knowledge of products and their availability.

Empathy and trust are essential for handling complaints and retaining customers. When solving problems for customers, the retail employee must comprehend the uniqueness of each situation while maintaining fair and equitable treatment for all customers. This requires flexibility in applying company policies and procedures so that the service provider satisfies customers while still working within corporate boundaries.

Here are some interventions that are particularly recommended for **retail** staff:

Awareness

2 Conjecture Lecture: First Impressions

4 It's a Jungle out There: Stereotyping

10 On the Line: Credibility

11 Power Up: Assertiveness

15 Meltdown: Dealing with Anger

Communication

19 Negative Ten-dency: Word Usage

20 Poker Face: Nonverbal Communication

33 Six Degrees of Persuasion: Influencing Through Listening

Planning

35 Commercial Appeal: Product or Service Offerings

37 Hardware: Classifying Resources

Problem Solving

58 Role It Out: Situational Role Play

59 Sensible Solutions: Alternative Solutions

Quality

69 Inconvenience Store: Service Strategies

72 Overcharged and Underrated: Exceeding Expectations

73 Picture Perfect: Communicating Quality

75 Right Approach: Service Attitude

80 Getting Down to Business: Customer Comment Cards

83 Concession Stand: Acknowledging Customer Concerns

Appendix D
Sales

Customers have become more sophisticated and responsible; they have less time and a more complicated environment in which to operate. This has far-reaching consequences for businesses that rely on sales contracts with their customers. A client establishes a long-term association with a company by building a rapport with its salespeople. The degree to which this connection exists depends on how satisfied the client is with the sale (transaction) and with how he or she is treated by the vendor (relationship). What customers need today are partners they can trust to understand their needs and problems, recommend the right solutions, and help them handle the details.

It is important for salespeople to lay the foundation for satisfaction by helping customers set realistic objectives and expectations for products or services. Customers are interested in what the services and products can do to help solve their problems or make life easier for them. Sales staff must transform the features and advantages of the company's offerings into terms a customer can understand, appreciate, and apply to his or her own situation. When this is done, salespeople build customer loyalty and ensure return business. It is critical that salespeople actively listen to what clients say and how they say it. That means having excellent communication skills to clearly and accurately articulate information and ideas, as well as to ask the right questions for determining customer needs.

Increased competition has encouraged specialization and diversification among products and services. Companies must be able to adapt, change course in midstream, and recognize opportunities before the competition does. Therefore, creativity is another critical part of building a base for customer satisfaction, enabling salespeople to generate new ways for customers to benefit from their company's products or services. No two customers are alike, and it is important to recognize the different needs, unique styles, and distinctive ideas of customers. The subsequent recommendations made by the salesperson must be made with confidence and self-assurance. An assertive person effectively influences, listens, and negotiates so that others choose to cooperate willing-ly. This win-win approach means that both parties end up with their needs met to the highest degree possible. When it comes to negotiating terms and conditions of a sale, the customer representative must work collaboratively with the client to negotiate a mutually acceptable deal that forms a partnership.

Establishing a relationship in which the customer not only obtains valuable products and services but *feels* as if he or she is getting value helps develop trust, a cornerstone of the sales transaction. To continue buying time and time again, the customer must be able to believe, and believe in, the salesperson. An essential component is for the representa-tive to establish personal commitment to the customer and always to act in the cus-tomer's best interests. In the end, clients want trust, credibility, reliability, responsiveness, and empathy from their sales representatives.

Here are some interventions that are particularly recommended for **sales** staff:

Awareness

6   Making Sense of It: Sensory Acuity

10   On the Line: Credibility

11   Power Up: Assertiveness

12   Flex Your Mind: Mental Flexibility

16   Plead Your Case: Influencing Change

Communication

20   Poker Face: Nonverbal Communication

22   Seeing Is Believing: Body Language and Culture

23   Summary Judgment: Listening

33   Six Degrees of Persuasion: Influencing Through Listening

Planning

35   Commercial Appeal: Product or Service Offerings

Problem Solving

61   Creativity Quotient: Self-Assessment

66   Fair Play: Win-Win Negotiation

67   Stage Right: Creative Process

Quality

73   Picture Perfect: Communicating Quality

76   Service Link: Creative Analysis of Service

77   Cream of the Crop: Quality Competencies

Teamwork

88   On Course: Communication, Reliability, and Trust

97   Rely on Me: Team Trust

About the Author

Lorraine L. Ukens, owner of Team-ing With Success (www.team-ing.com), is a performance improvement consultant who specializes in team building and experiential learning. Her business experience has been applied in designing, facilitating, and evaluating programs in a variety of areas. She has teamed with private companies, nonprofit organizations, and government agencies to help achieve higher levels of success.

Lorraine is the author of several training activity resources that make learning interactive and fun. These include activity books (*Getting Together, Working Together, All Together Now, Energize Your Audience, The New Encyclopedia of Group Activities, SkillBuilders: 50 Customer Service Activities,* and *Pump Them Up*), consensus simulations (*Adventure in the Amazon, Stranded in the Himalayas, Arctic Expedition, Trouble on the Inca Trail,* and *Lost in the Cradle of Gold*), and a training game (*Common Currency: The Cooperative-Competition Game*). She was the editor of *What Smart Trainers Know: The Secrets of Success from the World's Foremost Experts,* for which she wrote a chapter on team training. She also has contributed chapters to a variety of edited books ranging from team building to orientation.

Lorraine earned her B.S. degree in psychology and M.S. degree in human resource development from Towson University, near Baltimore, Maryland. She served as an adjunct faculty member in the graduate division at Towson from 1997 until 2005, when she moved to central Florida. She served as president of the Maryland Chapter of ASTD from 1999 to 2000 and continues to be active in the field of training and development.

How to Use the CD-ROM

- -

SYSTEM REQUIREMENTS

PC with Microsoft Windows 98SE or later
Mac with Apple OS version 8.6 or later

- -

USING THE CD WITH WINDOWS

To view the items located on the CD, follow these steps:

1. Insert the CD into your computer's CD-ROM drive.

2. A window appears with the following options:

   Contents: Allows you to view the files included on the CD-ROM.

   Software: Allows you to install useful software from the CD-ROM.

   Links: Displays a hyperlinked page of websites.

   Author: Displays a page with information about the author(s).

   Contact Us: Displays a page with information on contacting the publisher or author.

   Help: Displays a page with information on using the CD.

   Exit: Closes the interface window.

If you do not have autorun enabled, or if the autorun window does not appear, follow these steps to access the CD:

1. Click Start -> Run.

2. In the dialog box that appears, type d:\start.exe, where d is the letter of your CD-ROM drive. This brings up the autorun window described in the preceding set of steps.

3. Choose the desired option from the menu. (See Step 2 in the preceding list for a description of these options.)

IN CASE OF TROUBLE

If you experience difficulty using the CD-ROM, please follow these steps:

1. Make sure your hardware and systems configurations conform to the systems requirements noted under "System Requirements" above.

2. Review the installation procedure for your type of hardware and operating system. It is possible to reinstall the software if necessary.

To speak with someone in Product Technical Support, call 800-762-2974 or 317-572-3994 Monday through Friday from 8:30 a.m. to 5:00 p.m. EST. You can also contact Product Technical Support and get support information through our website at www.wiley.com/techsupport.

Before calling or writing, please have the following information available:

- Type of computer and operating system.

- Any error messages displayed.

- Complete description of the problem.

It is best if you are sitting at your computer when making the call.

Pfeiffer Publications Guide

This guide is designed to familiarize you with the various types of Pfeiffer publications. The formats section describes the various types of products that we publish; the methodologies section describes the many different ways that content might be provided within a product. We also provide a list of the topic areas in which we publish.

FORMATS

In addition to its extensive book-publishing program, Pfeiffer offers content in an array of formats, from fieldbooks for the practitioner to complete, ready-to-use training packages that support group learning.

FIELDBOOK Designed to provide information and guidance to practitioners in the midst of action. Most fieldbooks are companions to another, sometimes earlier, work, from which its ideas are derived; the fieldbook makes practical what was theoretical in the original text. Fieldbooks can certainly be read from cover to cover. More likely, though, you'll find yourself bouncing around following a particular theme, or dipping in as the mood, and the situation, dictate.

HANDBOOK A contributed volume of work on a single topic, comprising an eclectic mix of ideas, case studies, and best practices sourced by practitioners and experts in the field.

An editor or team of editors usually is appointed to seek out contributors and to evaluate content for relevance to the topic. Think of a handbook not as a ready-to-eat meal, but as a cookbook of ingredients that enables you to create the most fitting experience for the occasion.

RESOURCE Materials designed to support group learning. They come in many forms: a complete, ready-to-use exercise (such as a game); a comprehensive resource on one topic (such as conflict management) containing a variety of methods and approaches; or a collection of like-minded activities (such as icebreakers) on multiple subjects and situations.

TRAINING PACKAGE An entire, ready-to-use learning program that focuses on a particular topic or skill. All packages comprise a guide for the facilitator/trainer and a workbook for the participants. Some packages are supported with additional media—such as video—or learning aids, instruments, or other devices to help participants understand concepts or practice and develop skills.

- *Facilitator/trainer's guide* Contains an introduction to the program, advice on how to organize and facilitate the learning event, and step-by-step instructor notes. The guide also contains copies of presentation materials—handouts, presentations, and overhead designs, for example—used in the program.

- *Participant's workbook* Contains exercises and reading materials that support the learning goal and serves as a valuable reference and support guide for participants in the weeks and months that follow the learning event. Typically, each participant will require his or her own workbook.

ELECTRONIC CD-ROMs and web-based products transform static Pfeiffer content into dynamic, interactive experiences. Designed to take advantage of the searchability, automation, and ease-of-use that technology provides, our e-products bring convenience and immediate accessibility to your workspace.

METHODOLOGIES

CASE STUDY A presentation, in narrative form, of an actual event that has occurred inside an organization. Case studies are not prescriptive, nor are they used to prove a point; they are designed to develop critical analysis and decision-making skills. A case study has a specific time frame, specifies a sequence of events, is narrative in structure, and contains a plot structure—an issue (what should be/have been done?). Use case studies when the goal is to enable participants to apply previously learned theories to the circumstances in the case, decide what is pertinent, identify the real issues, decide what should have been done, and develop a plan of action.

ENERGIZER A short activity that develops readiness for the next session or learning event. Energizers are most commonly used after a break or lunch to stimulate or refocus the group. Many involve some form of physical activity, so they are a useful way to counter post-lunch lethargy. Other uses include transitioning from one topic to another, where "mental" distancing is important.

EXPERIENTIAL LEARNING ACTIVITY (ELA) A facilitator-led intervention that moves participants through the learning cycle from experience to application (also known as a Structured Experience). ELAs are carefully thought-out designs in which there is a definite learning purpose and intended outcome. Each step—everything that participants do during the activity—facilitates the accomplishment of the stated goal. Each ELA includes complete instructions for facilitating the intervention and a clear statement of goals, suggested group size and timing, materials required, an explanation of the process, and, where appropriate, possible variations to the activity. (For more detail on Experiential Learning Activities, see the Introduction to the *Reference Guide to Handbooks and Annuals*, 1999 edition, Pfeiffer, San Francisco.)

GAME A group activity that has the purpose of fostering team spirit and togetherness in addition to the achievement of a pre-stated goal. Usually contrived—undertaking a desert expedition, for example—this type of learning method offers an engaging means for participants to demonstrate and practice business and interpersonal skills. Games are effective for team building and personal development mainly because the goal is subordinate to the process—the means through which participants reach decisions, collaborate, communicate, and generate trust and understanding. Games often engage teams in "friendly" competition.

ICEBREAKER A (usually) short activity designed to help participants overcome initial anxiety in a training session and/or to acquaint the participants with one another. An icebreaker can be a fun activity or can be tied to specific topics or training goals. While a useful tool in itself, the icebreaker comes into its own in situations where tension or resistance exists within a group.

INSTRUMENT A device used to assess, appraise, evaluate, describe, classify, and summarize various aspects of human behavior. The term used to describe an instrument depends primarily on its format and purpose. These terms include survey, questionnaire, inventory, diagnostic, survey, and poll. Some uses of instruments include providing instrumental feedback to group members, studying here-and-now processes or functioning within a group, manipulating group composition, and evaluating outcomes of training and other interventions.

Instruments are popular in the training and HR field because, in general, more growth can occur if an individual is provided with a method for focusing specifically on his or her own behavior. Instruments also are used to obtain information that will serve as a basis for change and to assist in workforce planning efforts.

Paper-and-pencil tests still dominate the instrument landscape with a typical package comprising a facilitator's guide, which offers advice on administering the instrument and interpreting the collected data, and an initial set of instruments. Additional instruments are available separately. Pfeiffer, though, is investing heavily in e-instruments. Electronic instrumentation provides effortless distribution and, for larger groups particularly, offers advantages over paper-and-pencil tests in the time it takes to analyze data and provide feedback.

LECTURETTE A short talk that provides an explanation of a principle, model, or process that is pertinent to the participants' current learning needs. A lecturette is intended to establish a common language bond between the trainer and the participants by providing a mutual frame of reference. Use a lecturette as an introduction to a group activity or event, as an interjection during an event, or as a handout.

MODEL A graphic depiction of a system or process and the relationship among its elements. Models provide a frame of reference and something more tangible, and more easily remembered, than a verbal explanation. They also give participants something to "go on," enabling them to track their own progress as they experience the dynamics, processes, and relationships being depicted in the model.

ROLE PLAY A technique in which people assume a role in a situation/scenario: a customer service rep in an angry-customer exchange, for example. The way in which the role is approached is then discussed and feedback is offered. The role play is often repeated using a different approach and/or incorporating changes made based on feedback received. In other words, role playing is a spontaneous interaction involving realistic behavior under artificial (and safe) conditions.

SIMULATION A methodology for understanding the interrelationships among components of a system or process. Simulations differ from games in that they test or use a model that depicts or mirrors some aspect of reality in form, if not necessarily in content. Learning occurs by studying the effects of change on one or more factors of the model. Simulations are commonly used to test hypotheses about what happens in a system—often referred to as "what if?" analysis—or to examine best-case/worst-case scenarios.

THEORY A presentation of an idea from a conjectural perspective. Theories are useful because they encourage us to examine behavior and phenomena through a different lens.

TOPICS

The twin goals of providing effective and practical solutions for workforce training and organization development and meeting the educational needs of training and human resource professionals shape Pfeiffer's publishing program. Core topics include the following:

Leadership & Management

Communication & Presentation

Coaching & Mentoring

Training & Development

E-Learning

Teams & Collaboration

OD & Strategic Planning

Human Resources

Consulting

What will you find on pfeiffer.com?

- The best in workplace performance solutions for training and HR professionals

- Downloadable training tools, exercises, and content

- Web-exclusive offers

- Training tips, articles, and news

- Seamless on-line ordering

- Author guidelines, information on becoming a Pfeiffer Affiliate, and much more

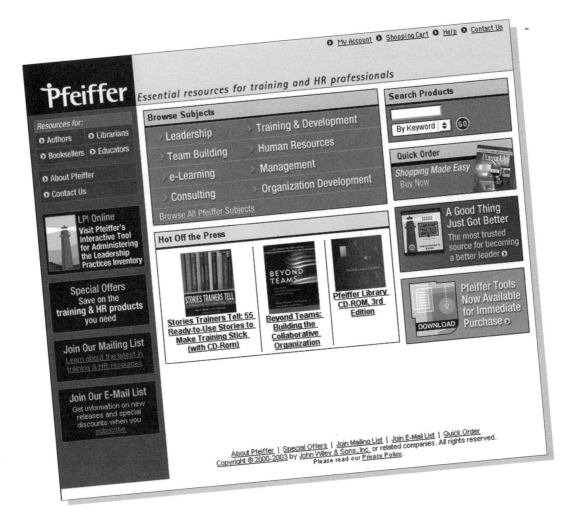

Discover more at www.pfeiffer.com